A PRACTICAL APPROACH TO TEACHING

FOUNDATIONAL
READING SKILLS

IN THE CLASSROOM AND AT HOME
STRATEGIES FOR TEACHERS AND PARENTS
REVISED EDITION

Foreword By
Dr. Marquita S. Blades

Dr. Daphne Coleman
Dr. Char-Shenda Covington
Shanell Lee, Ed.S.
Cynthia Logan, M.Ed.
Mysha McClain, M.Ed.
Dr. Elondra D. Napper

Fleri Publishing

Copyright ©2021 Fleri Publishing, LLC.
Published by Fleri Publishing, LLC.
Lithia Springs, GA 30122
www.fleribookpublishing.com
shanell.lee@fleribookpublishing.com

Library of Congress Control Number: 2020925113
ISBN: 978-1-7352493-1-5

Printed in the U.S.A.

ACKNOWLEDGEMENTS

Fleri Publishing, Shanell Lee, and the contributing authors of *A Practical Approach to Teaching Foundational Reading Skills* would like to thank the following contributors and reviewers:

Bonus Strategy Contributors

Larue M. Fitch, M.Ed.
Educational Consultant & Author,
Breaking the Education Code

Dee Harris
Master Educator & Founder, The
Skillful Learner

Dr. Sheva Quinn
Educator, Author, & Business Coach
Founder, Black Classical University

Quatia Stevens
Educator & Author
Owner, SCA Tutoring

Dr. Tricia Y. Travis
Educator
CEO Celebrity Educator

Book Reviewers

Chike Akua, Ph.D.
Assistant Professor of Educational
Leadership, Clark Atlanta University &
Author, *Education for Transformation*

Dr. Johni Cruse-Craig
Educator, Advocate, Mentor &
Business Coach

Vincent Taylor, M.Ed.
Educator
Author of *Cornbread* Children's
Book Series

ABOUT THE AUTHORS

 **Daphne Grant Coleman, Ed. D** is an Instructional Coach focused on reading and literacy at an elementary school in Atlanta, Georgia. Her duties include improving and enhancing Tier I reading instruction by observing teachers, modeling lessons, and providing feedback and professional development to ensure that those closest to our students are prepared with the knowledge, skills and materials to provide students with a valuable learning experience and improve academic achievement. Dr. Coleman is a career educator with 30 years of experience. During her career she has served as a teacher working with all elementary grades, Instructional Liaison Specialist, Reading Facilitator, and Reading Specialist. In her various roles, she has acquired a myriad of knowledge and skills that she is excited to share.

Dr. Coleman earned a bachelor's degree from the University of Georgia, a master's degree from Georgia State University and a doctorate and leadership certification from the University of West Georgia. In addition to her formal education, she has gifted and reading endorsements. Dr. Coleman has been married for 28 years and has three children – Camryn, a graduate of Georgia Southern University; Christian, a professional track and field athlete and graduate from the University of Tennessee; and Cailyn, a student at Livingstone College. Dr. Coleman is a member of Alpha Kappa Alpha Sorority, activist working with the PTSA, and a Servant Leader in the youth ministry at Elizabeth Baptist Church. In her spare time, she enjoys playing games, dining out and spending time with family.

Dr.Char-Shenda Covington, Ph.D, Ed. D is currently serving as a turnaround principal in the third largest school district in GA. Her 15 years in education have provided her the opportunity to gain experience in supporting the executive/instructional leadership teams in schools across the nation. She has created, developed, and monitored the effective implementation of state standards, evaluated the quality of teaching and learning, and created assessments at the school and district levels. Dr. Covington served as a School Improvement Consultant and Literacy Trainer with the Southern Regional Education Board (SREB) in Atlanta, GA in which she primarily served the bottom 5% of schools in 14 states. She is the owner of Academic Literacy Services, LLC., with the primary goal of assisting adult learners with completion of their academic studies. Dr. Covington has also been an assistant principals, chief academic officers, curriculum directors, and assessment developers at the state and district levels.

Dr. Covington is a proud member of the Order of Eastern Star and Delta Sigma Theta Sorority, Inc. For the last 6 years, she has been an active participant with the Delta Teacher Efficacy Campaign (DTEC). DTEC supports teachers in an effort to enhance the educational opportunities for minority students throughout the country. This partnership with Delta Sigma Theta Sorority and the Bill & Melinda Gates Foundation has a three-pronged approach which includes training teachers, advocacy, and publishing scholarly research on teacher efficacy and student achievement. Dr. Covington's contributions included the co-publication, of *Beyond the Surface: Examining Leadership's Role in Collective Efficacy*. She is happy to be amongst those who are a voice for equity!

Dr. Covington has received numerous awards and/or recognition as an agent of change in the field of Education. She formerly served as a member of the Social Studies Steering committee for Governor Deal, in conjunction with the Georgia Department of Education, was the youngest graduate for both her masters and doctoral programs, as well as a recipient of the Principal's Awards from each school employed.

Dr. Covington holds a Bachelors of Arts in Political Science from Spelman College, a Masters of Education in Curriculum and Instruction from Central Michigan University, and a Doctorate of Education (PhD) from Capella University with a specialization in Educational Leadership and Administration. In the spring of 2016, she completed her second doctorate, a Doctorate of Education (EdD) from Northcentral University specializing in Organizational Leadership, with a focus on School Improvement. As a first-generation college graduate, she prides herself on being a passionate voice for all students, regardless of their societal constructs, letting them know they have the ability and capacity to succeed, no matter the odds. Her educational philosophy is simple, "All students can learn and teachers can teach when equipped with the necessary tools." Dr. Covington enjoys reading, cooking, and dancing with her daughter.

Shanell Lee, Ed.S. is a bestselling author, award-winning educator, and publisher. Over the past fourteen years in education, she has served in the capacity of classroom teacher, Reading Specialist, and Professional Development Leader. Ms. Lee's areas of focus are writing in the primary grades, foundational reading skills, guided reading, and reading in the content areas. She continually stresses the importance of supporting students' development of foundational reading skills in primary grades so that they can become strong readers that are able to access text in all content areas with minimal challenges.

Lee has dedicated her career to encouraging and inspiring people to take control of their lives through education. Her own teachers and professors had a profound impact on this life's mission. Her journey to help others began as a high school teacher and continues to this day, as she works to make a positive difference in many children's lives as an elementary school educator. Her educational background includes an Ed.S in Education Leadership from Barry University, a M.S in Public Administration from the University of Phoenix, and a B.S in Business Administration from Nova Southeastern University. She is a highly resourceful, results-driven educator with a proven commitment to implementing research-based instructional practices and programs that promote quality teaching and increased academic achievement in public school settings.

Cynthia Logan. M.Ed. is the oldest of four children, and thus, she was tasked with helping her younger siblings with homework and daily life skills. In doing this she discovered that teaching was her gift. Coupled with her education, Mrs. Logan attributes her success to her natural, God-given talents.

Mrs. Logan earned her B.S. in Early Childhood Special Education from Mercer University and a MA in Education with an emphasis in Curriculum and Instruction from Capella University. Her instructional certificate includes Reading, Gifted, and Special Educational endorsements. During her seven-year tenure in classrooms both abroad and in metro Atlanta school districts, she served as a General Education and a Special Education teacher. She remembers those classroom experiences where she empowered young children and encouraged them to stretch themselves through practical, engaging, and cognitive exercises as being the most rewarding of her career.

In 2015, she took her skillset global, accepting a position in the United Arab Emirates with the Abu Dhabi Educational Counsel. Finding herself leading classes of twenty-eight 1st-graders and twenty 5th-graders,

she had to rely on her pedagogy to ensure her students' success. Mrs. Logan was named the English

Language Lead for the cycle one (elementary level).

Currently, she has transitioned from the classroom and is advocating for both African American and immigrant teens and educators without the confounds of educational bureaucracy through her nonprofit organization, Nourishing Hands Inc.

 **Dr. Elondra D. Napper** is an award-winning best-selling author, STREAMA (Science Technology Reading Engineering Arts, Music, Math and Agriculture) Educator and consultant for Encouraging Champions Consulting Firm. Dr. Napper has served in schools across the country for the last for 23 years as a teacher assistant, teacher, instructional coach, assistant principal, principal, teaching assistant professor, researcher, and consultant. Dr. Napper is a children's book author who uses science standards and inquiry to teach scholars about science concepts while building their self-esteem! Her most recent books include *My Name is Rona! The Quarantine Chronicles, Every Child Needs a Champion* and *Chloe the Confident Caterpillar*.

Dr. Napper supports educators and educational leaders by teaching them how to incorporate science and guided reading instruction in elementary and middle school classrooms using her curriculum and pedagogical model for teaching and learning called Science is LiT: Science Looks Like Me. Using evidence-based strategies and elements of instructional design, she supports educator's development by using vocabulary, guided reading components and science inquiry into a lab environment to close the knowledge and culturally responsive gap while incorporating social-emotional strategies.

She has recently launched Champions STREAMA Academy, an online school for students to learn STREAMA (Science Technology Reading Engineering Arts, Music, Math and Agriculture). She is in the process of creating an online space to support teachers and administrators to receive professional development to support Professional Learning Communities specifically focused on instructional leadership, culturally responsive pedagogy and social-emotional learning. Dr. Napper believes that every child needs a champion and it is her mission to encourage educators to exercise the champion in them so they can build champion scholars in their classrooms and schools.

**Mysha McClain, M.Ed.** is an educator, advocate, an entrepreneur. Mysha has 14 years of experience working with scholars in pre-K through 12th grade. She has earned a Master of Education degree in administrative leadership from Sierra Nevada University and bachelor's degrees in elementary education and special education from Nevada State College. She has made many contributions to education by teaching scholars, advocating in the community, developing policies, leading teams, and training parents and teachers.

1n 2016, Mysha was recognized as teacher of the year for her hard work and dedication in educating at-risk kindergarten scholars. As a regular education teacher, Mysha was praised for her abilities to differentiate instruction, address social-emotional needs of students, and provide students with solid foundations in reading and math. Mysha's passion for teaching all scholars, led her back to special education where she served as a special education facilitator for K-8 students where she was able to transform the special education department at two schools and positively increase scholar achievement.

In 2018, Mysha served as master cadre for training educators on social-emotional interventions where she used the pyramid model to support teachers in applying appropriate practices for supporting positive social-emotional skills. This work has led her to providing many public speaking engagements and develop state policies to support all students, with an emphasis on individuals with challenging behaviors and/or disabilities. In 2019, Mysha was acknowledged for her efforts by the National Celebrity Educator organization as the Nevada Celebrity Educator of the Year. As the Nevada Celebrity Educator of the year, Mysha has collaborated with many educators from across the United States to make positive changes in education. In 2020, Mysha founded McClain Education Consultation, where she provides consultation to schools and districts to increase scholar achievement by addressing the achievement gap, addressing implicit biases, and using data to inform decisions. Mysha continues to do her part in education to ensure student growth and success.

ABOUT THE EDITOR

 **Dr. Marquita S. Blades** is an award-winning STEM Educator and Teacher EmPOWARRment Specialist with 16 years of experience as a high school science teacher and manager of national STEM programs. Dr. Blades is currently a full-time Education Consultant, author, and publisher. She is the owner of Dr. Blades Consulting, LLC which offers professional development programs, curriculum and assessment writing, conference programming, and teacher coaching services.

Dr. Blades saves schools, school districts, and other educational programs time and money by teaching them to increase student engagement through rigorous and meaningful learning experiences using the resources they already have on-hand. Her signature program, *POWARRful* Teaching Strategies® includes two highly-engaging national PD workshops: Practical Implementation of the Next Generation Science Standards and *POWARRful* Teaching Strategies® for Increasing Student Engagement.

Dr. Blades is a contributing author for *The Whole Truth Anthology* which was released in 2017, the lead author for Amazon best-selling anthology, *The Mediocre Teacher Project*, and *POWARRful Teaching Strategies® for Increasing Engagement*. She contributed to EduMatch's *Snapshot in Education 2019*. She is also the author of several resource manuals on teaching the Next Generation Science Standards.

Dr. Blades is a member of Sigma Gamma Rho Sorority, Inc. and The National Sorority of Phi Delta Kappa. She has received numerous awards for her service to the community and in the field of education.

Dr. Blades holds a BIS in Broad Field Science from Georgia State University, an MS in Technical and Professional Communication from Southern Polytechnic State University, and an Ed.D. in Instructional Leadership from Nova Southeastern University. Dr. Blades enjoys reading, cooking, and traveling with her husband. Learn more about Dr. Blades by visiting www.drmarquitablades.com

FOREWORD

I've said many times: "*I'm not a reading teacher*", but the fact of the matter is that *all* teachers are reading teachers. As a STEM Educator in both public schools and private educational programs for 20 years, I have encountered many students, even those who are high-achievers, who experience academic deficits that are directly linked to their reading comprehension skills.

Over the years, explicit vocabulary instruction has become less and less of a priority in the upper grades, yet students must rely on their reading comprehension skills more and more. Teaching vocabulary explicitly has been eliminated from a lot of middle and high school classrooms and replaced with what are considered to be "better" activities aimed at helping students increase their knowledge of subject-matter words and their meanings. In elementary school, students learn to read, and in high school, they read to learn. In high school, students must rely on their reading skills in order to be successful in the content areas. If students don't have a strong foundation in reading, this is not possible.

Reading is the foundation upon which all other learning relies. Even in the most collaborative and engaging classes, there will be times when students have to rely on their own reading skills to accomplish assigned tasks. If we have learned nothing at all during the COVID-19 pandemic, we have certainly learned that students need be able to function independently, especially in virtual learning spaces. In order to function independently, students will need to read and interpret information without their teacher's assistance.

High-level instruction can be crippled if the teacher does not address the underlying issues that students face with their reading skills. As a result, a content area teacher may end up teaching prefixes and suffixes, summarization, visualization, and a host of other skills that students may not have learned as beginning readers — not to the extent of a teacher who specializes in reading instruction — but they have to teach these things nonetheless, lest their students are hindered from learning any subject matter.

Since all teachers have to do this work, all teachers deserve quality resources to support them in doing so. This book provides the essentials of teaching foundational reading skills that any and all teachers need. Not only that, the book is written for parents who want to provide the additional support that their children need to become strong readers. With people becoming more isolated and working remotely, there is a growing need for more educators and at-home teachers, i.e., parents, to be able to provide the type of reading instruction that will produce learners who have a love for proficient and fluent reading that allows them to function independently. In this book, you'll find research-based, classroom-tested strategies presented in a practical way that can be implemented immediately in the classroom and at home.

CONTENTS

INTRODUCTION

Literacy is the bedrock for all instruction that takes place. This is inclusive of not only the core content areas of English/Language Arts, Mathematics, Science, Social Studies, but also Art, Music, Physical Education, etc. The current educational landscape, regarding America's literacy rate, highlights issues with the cultural achievement and opportunity gaps. Green and Goldstein (2019) reported that 4th and 8th grade students struggle to read on-level academic texts and that 67% of students fail to meet reading proficiency standards, as measured by the National Assessment of Educational Progress. Furthermore, they shared the average 8th graders' reading scores declined in more than 25 states, since 2017, along with 4th graders' scores declining in 17 states (Green & Goldstein, 2019). A shift is necessary. The quality of literacy-rich environments must be at the forefront of legislation and teaching and learning.

The need to increase student achievement is at the core of school improvement (Covington, 2016). Framing reading literacy, within the American school system, is a necessity to ensure students' ability to function as responsible citizens. Students must leave each grade level proficient in reading, based on the state's standards. Students are in dire need of culturally responsive leaders and teachers, who embrace literacy instruction and are knowledgeable about the impact that literacy in the earlier years has on the opportunities that students will have upon completion of high school. It is critical to equip students with the necessary tools to ensure they are not only able to read, but able to think critically about what is happening around them, and that starts with effective strategies to address foundational skills evidenced in phonemic awareness, phonics, comprehension, vocabulary, and fluency.

During my fifteen years of serving as a classroom teacher and a reading specialist, I've had the opportunity to teach and support proficient, as well as, struggling readers. I often found myself reflecting on the notes collected during my guided reading groups and wondered how I could better help my students overcome their challenges.

You may have heard educators say "in kindergarten through second grade, students learn to read, and in third through fifth grade, students read to learn." Early grade students learn to read by engaging in instruction focused on phonemic awareness, phonics, vocabulary, and fluency. However, instructional time is also relegated to teaching literacy and informational standards, along with writing. So, students must also "with prompting and support" engage with rigorous texts. This means comprehension is a focus in kindergarten through second grade classrooms too.

Teachers provide instruction and track student growth with the use of curricula like Fountas and Pinell, Scholastic, and Reading Recovery, which offer leveled texts. At the beginning of the year and periodically thereafter, students are assessed and identified as reading at, above, or below grade level. This continues through fifth grade. School leaders and teachers are able to monitor student growth this way.

In third through fifth grade classrooms, there is an increased focus on comprehension of literary and informational text, which spans across content areas. Once again, we are faced with the presupposition that before students can gain comprehension of what they're reading, they must be somewhat proficient readers. The rigor of standards-based instruction and grade-level assessments allows teachers to identify students that face challenges when trying to access grade-level text and indicates when additional instructional support is needed.

Students need a certain level of proficiency in phonemic awareness, phonics, vocabulary, and fluency so that they can concentrate on the meaning of the texts they are reading and less on decoding them. Our motivation for this book stems from the overwhelming need of support for young and struggling readers from educators within the school and their caregivers at home.

This book was designed to provide pre-service teachers, current practitioners, and parents who've elected to extend student learning at home, a practical approach to teaching reading foundational skills to students in pre-kindergarten through fifth grade.

Each chapter provides:

- Explanations of foundational reading skills and the importance of students obtaining proficiency in each skill
- Practical Strategies to teach reading foundational skills in the classroom
- Practical Strategies to teach reading foundational skills at home
- Resources to support teaching and learning of each foundational reading skill

How to Use this Book

There are two ways to use this book. The first way is to begin with chapter one and read it in sequence. As you read about each foundational reading skill, you can incorporate the strategies within your instruction. Another way to use this book is to be strategic and start where your needs lie. For example, if you have a reader that struggles with vocabulary, you may start with chapter 3 and learn the importance of the foundational skill and practical strategies to implement within the classroom or at home to support student growth.

Also, seek out resources available to benefit or maintain teaching and learning. As your students begins to progress, you will find yourself switching between different chapters to find practical teaching strategies to employ, in order to aid your students' journey in becoming better readers. Lastly, it is our goal for this book to provide educators, and parents alike, practical strategies they can employ effectively and efficiently to support student learning and positively impact the reading achievement of students.

CHAPTER ONE

PHONEMIC AWARENESS

Learning to read involves a very specific set of foundational skills beginning with phonemic awareness and then phonics, vocabulary, fluency, and comprehension, respectively. While is it not practical to believe that all students will always acquire these skills in this is order prior to being exposed to and expected to use the others, research has shown that when taught in sequence, these skills lead to the development of proficient readers. Each skill builds upon the one that comes before, therefore, the foundation must be solid. That foundation begins with phonemic awareness.

Phonological awareness is a broad skill that includes identifying and manipulating units of oral language-parts such as words, syllables, and onsets and rimes. **Phonemic** awareness refers to the specific ability to focus on and manipulate individual sounds (phonemes) in spoken words. Building a child's understanding and application of phonological and phonemic of awareness will set the course for their reading achievement. When students develop phonological and phonemic awareness, it allows them to practice decoding words. Decoding is critical to reading development and will be discussed in greater detail later. When students practice decoding, they can isolate and blend each sound to pronounce the word. The more they practice this skill the more their fluency and comprehension skills will improve as well. Research shows that students who have difficulty with reading comprehension as they progress through the grade levels is directly correlated to the student's development, or the lack thereof, of phonemic and phonological awareness (Reading Rockets, 2020).

Phonological Awareness

Phonological awareness is an understanding that spoken language is broken into smaller units. Phonological awareness includes using sound-related skills that are necessary for a child to grow as a reader. Table 1.1 identifies each phonological skill that students will need to develop in order to improve and/or increase their reading skills. Table 1.1 also explains how each phonological skill translates into the development of decoding sounds and letters to create words. In summation, phonological awareness includes sounds that transform into letters. Letters put together form words. Words put together form sentences. Sentences form paragraphs, and multiple paragraphs on multiple pages build texts.

Phonemic Awareness

Phonemic awareness is defined as the ability to hear sounds in oral language. The fundamental part of teaching a child to read starts with a sound. Every letter in the English alphabet has a sound. The basic unit of sound is called a **phoneme**, so phonemes are the smallest unit of sound in the English language. Phonemes help the reader distinguish one word or meaning from another word or meaning. For example, there are forty-four phonemes and twenty-six letters in the alphabet. Having the ability to distinguish between sounds is correlated to being able to pronounce words and understand their meanings.

Phonemic awareness skills support a child's decoding development. Decoding is a process in which the printed word is pronounced correctly by isolating each phoneme. Ultimately, students' phonemic awareness skills will impact their abilities to comprehend text as they develop as readers. Therefore, it is imperative that teachers and parents help children develop phonemic awareness.

When students develop the skill of isolating the sounds of letters, then phonemic awareness can be used as a strong predictor of a student's reading ability and an indicator of the student's success as a reader. Think of phonemic awareness, one of the building blocks of reading development, as a set of stairs (See Figure 1.1). The base of the stairs is phonological awareness. On the first step is rhyming and alliteration. The second step is sentence segmentation. The third step is syllables. The fourth step includes onsets and rimes, and the fifth step is phonemic awareness. "The goal of reading is to be able to both decode and comprehend text. Once kids can decode words well, they can begin to work on remembering and understanding the words they are reading." (Sheakoski, 2014).

Table 1.1 Phonological Skills Required for Developing Reading Skills

Phonological Skills	Explanation/Example of Skill
Word Awareness	☐ The ability to discriminate between individual words **Example:** Read a sentence as the learner follows along on the page. As each word is read, the learner covers the word with a coin or other object.
Syllables	☐ Words broken down into smaller parts **Example:** The word **clapping** has two syllables (also referred to as chunks): **Syllable1:** /Clap/ **Chunk 2:** /ing/
Onsets	☐ The beginning sounds of words **Example:** The beginning sound in the word **clap**ping is **/clap/**
Rimes	☐ The ending sounds of words **Example:** The ending sound in the word clap**ping** is **/ing/**
Phonemes	☐ The smallest unit of sound in the spoken word **Example:** The word **ball** has **three** phonemes: | Phoneme #1 /b/	Phoneme #2 /aw/	Phoneme #3 /l/	

Figure 1.1 Phonemic Awareness Stairs

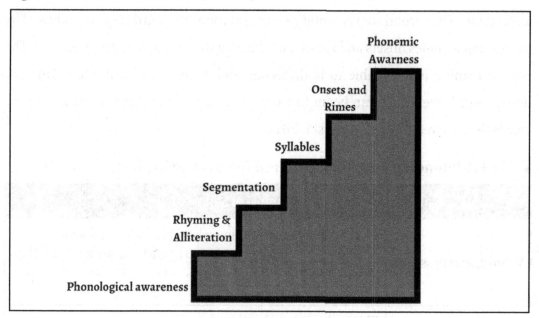

Reading is not a skill that is developed naturally. Reading must be taught explicitly and systematically for children to become literate. Kamhi (2007) eloquently describes the differences between decoding (word recognition) and comprehension. Decoding is "a teachable skill" compared to comprehension, which "is not a skill and is not easily taught." Kamhi explains that word recognition is a teachable skill because it "involves a narrow scope of knowledge (e.g. letters, sounds, words) and processes (decoding) that, once acquired, will lead to fast, accurate word recognition" (Kamhi, 2007).

Approach to Teaching Phonemic Awareness in Classroom

Strong phonemic awareness and phonological awareness is a good predictor of a student's reading ability. If a student struggles with reading comprehension, then it can be deducted that they also have weak phonemic and phonological awareness skills. According to Blachman, "Students with strong phonological awareness are likely to become good readers, but students with weak phonological skills will likely become poor readers (2000). It is estimated that the vast majority—more than 90 percent—of students with significant reading problems have a core deficit in their ability to process phonological information" (Blachman, 1995).

Table 1.2 includes instructional strategies to incorporate when teaching phonemic awareness in the classroom. These phonemic awareness strategies can be implemented in centers, during direct instruction, or as a warmup activity prior to instruction. These strategies can be used as a way to progress monitor student's growth and development in regard to phonemic and phonological awareness skills.

Approach to Teaching Phonemic Awareness at Home

Parents and guardians are a child's first teacher. Table 1.3 summarizes how parents and guardians can support and assess the development of phonemic and phonological awareness with their children at home. It is also recommended that parents and guardians assist their children with creating a notebook to document the strategies that are being used during their reading time. In this notebook, parents and guardians should record if their child is having difficulties with any of the following skills as identified by the National Center on Improving Literacy (2017):

- Noticing and naming rhymes
- Noticing and playing with individual sounds in spoken words
- Quickly naming aloud a series of familiar items, like letters, numbers, or colors
- Sounding out unknown words
- Reading "like you talk" instead of word by word (reading with expression)
- Remembering the ideas in a story
- Spelling words correctly

Table 1.2 Instructional Strategies for Teaching Phonemic Awareness in the Classroom

Strategy		How to Implement Strategy
Deleting a sound		Ask students to listen to words and say the word without the first sound.
Adding Phonemes		Ask students to listen to a word and add a syllable. **Example:** Add *-ing* to a word cook to make *cooking*
Substituting Phonemes		Change a phoneme in a word. **Example:** Change the vowel /o/ in the word d<u>o</u>g with the vowel / i / now the word has changed from dog to dig.
Transposing Phonemes		Reverse the sounds in a word. **Example:** Change the /p/ and the /t/ in the word **pot** the new word is /t/ /o/ /p/ = **top**.
Listening and Visual Discrimination		Match pictures to sounds and letters.
Segmentation		Use **Elkonin Boxes** to teach students how to isolate each phoneme. **Example:** |		
		| ☐ Write or place a cut-out letter in each box. ☐ The student says the word and counts the number of phonemes. For example, C-A-T has three phonemes. ☐ As the child says each letter, they slide a cube or letters into each box separately demonstrating their understanding of each sound and the number of phonemes in the word.

Table 1.3 Instructional Strategies for Teaching Phonemic Awareness at Home

Strategy	How to Implement Strategy
Listening Games	Read nursey rhymes aloud and have the child identify the rhyming words and the beginning (onset) and ending (rime) sounds of the word.
Rhyming Activities	Engage the child in a rhyming scavenger hunt. **Say:** I see something in the (room, car, etc.) that rhymes with star. The child must state a word that rhymes with the spoken word.
Syllable Awareness Activities	Model how to identify the number of syllables in a word by clapping. **Example:** If a word has two syllables (chunks), the child would clap their hands twice to demonstrate the number of syllables in the word.
Letter Introduction and Spelling Practice	☐ Chose a letter. ☐ Model the letter for the child by saying the letter of the object that you have located. ☐ Ask the child to locate something in the room that starts with a particular letter. ☐ The child will identify all the objects in the room that start with that letter.

If these skills are not the issue, that may mean there could be something else that has been overlooked, such as hearing and/or vision problems. If your child is not experiencing challenges with the skills in the list above, then checking their hearing and vision could be the next step in helping your child with reading. If a child is having hearing challenges, it will impact their ability to distinguish between sounds, which impacts their phonemic and phonological awareness. If the child is having vision challenges, then they will have difficulty with distinguishing between letters. The connection between letter and sound recognition is critical for reading development.

Teaching Phonemic Awareness in Digital/Virtual/Blended Learning Environments

Teaching students to read and supporting literacy development in digital/virtual learning environments is not as simple as transferring printed materials to virtual space. One of the barriers, researchers have found, is that students don't comprehend online text as deeply as printed materials" (Fingal, 2020). Students tend to skim over digital text quickly rather than taking the time to interact with the text. Fingal also suggests that students are distracted when reading online. When feasible, books in print will always be the best resource to support reading development.

Educators must create or adapt the strategies they use to support reading instruction in online learning environments. Teachers can make sure that they slow down the pace of instruction, use educational technology tools to promote student engagement online, engage students in discussions online, and plan for reflection activities. One educational technology tool to include is the Google Docs highlighting feature to emphasize key points in the lesson. Also, learners will still benefit from using paper and pencil to take notes and to reflect. The goal of using this or similar strategies is to help the learner shift their tendency to skim text online.

Conclusion

Reading is the ability to extract meaning from text. When students have developed phonemic and phonological awareness skills, then they can begin to understand how the sounds in spoken language make words and how words are containers of meaning and knowledge. "Research shows that when schools, teachers, and families are well-informed, children make greater gains in reading and writing" (National Center on Improving Literacy, 2017). When teachers deliver instruction at school along with the support that parents provide at home, children are being prepared to begin applying their understanding of decoding, isolating sounds in words, to start phonics instruction. Table 1.4 lists several resources that are beneficial to both teachers and parents in providing quality phonemic awareness instruction in the classroom and at home.

Table 1.4 Resources to Support Phonemic Awareness Instruction in the Classroom and at Home

Title of Resource	URL	Description
Phonemic Awareness: An Introduction	https://www.readingrockets.org/article/phonemic-awareness-introduction	This article is written by the Partnership for Reading that introduces the skill of phonemic awareness. The article includes how children can demonstrate their understanding of how to recognize phonemes.
Shanahan on Literacy	https://shanahanonliteracy.com/	This website includes articles about the science of reading development and links to literacy websites, articles, and books.
International Literacy Association	https://www.literacyworldwide.org/	This website includes resources, and information about meetings and events to empower teachers and parents to support literacy development.
Read Write Think	http://www.readwritethink.org/about/our-partners/international-literacy-association-1.html	This website includes resources, and information about meetings and events to empower teachers and parents to support literacy development.
Literacy Research Association	https://www.literacyresearchassociation.org/	This website includes resources, and information about meetings and events to empower teachers and parents to support literacy development.
Starfall	https://www.starfall.com/h/	Starfall is an online program that teaches children how to read in a collaborative fun learning experience for grades K-3.
ABCYA	https://www.abcya.com/	ABCYA is a website with educational games for kids.
Reading Eggs	https://readingeggs.com/	Reading Eggs is a website with fun and interactive reading games and activities that are based on scientific research.

CHAPTER TWO

PHONICS

In the previous chapter you were given some practical suggestions for teaching children about letters and their individual sounds, and how they can manipulate those sounds to comprise words. Next, instruction should help children build upon their understanding of phonemes and delve into a more complex usage of letters and sounds utilizing phonics - the building blocks of reading and writing. Parents, educators, reading researchers, and policymakers all agree that children must learn to read to participate fully in a modern society. They agree, moreover, that much of this learning will take place in school.

There have been many debates about how children should learn to read. Debates between proponents of phonics instruction and proponents of whole-language instruction have sometimes been so heated that they have been called the "reading wars." What can psychological science tell us about this issue? This is the question that (Castles, Rastle, and Nation, 2018) set out to answer, in providing a wide-ranging review of how reading skills are developed from beginners to expert level, and considerations of the implications of the research for how reading should be taught.

What is Phonics?

Phonics is the method of teaching reading by correlating sounds with letters or groups of letters in an alphabetic writing system. Phonics instruction teaches readers how to decode letters into their respective sounds, a skill that is an essential prerequisite for learning how to read the 44 phonics sounds in the English language.

Scientific studies have found that explicit systematic phonics instruction is the most effective way to teach children how to read.

Over the years the term *phonics* has had many definitions. Based on my professional experience, there is irrefutable evidence that supports phonics as a foundational skill that must be acquired in order for an individual to be a proficient reader and to speak effectively in English. Phonics instruction is an attempt to provide the guidance and intentional teaching that children need to learn how the alphabetic writing system works.

The Difficulty of Reading and the Importance of Phonics Instruction

Reading is, in the words of (Gough and Hillinger, 1980), an unnatural act. It is particularly unnatural when its represented by individual speech sounds, as in alphabetic writing systems. Adults who know how to read and write an alphabet find it obvious that spoken words are composed of sounds. But these things are not obvious to preliterate children, illiterate adults, or adults who are literate in a non-alphabetic writing system (Liberman, Shankweiler, Fischer, & Carter, 1974; Morais, Cary, Alegria, & Bettelson, 1979; Read, Zhang, Nie, & Ding, 1986). Individual speech sounds, what linguists call *phonemes*, are abstract units.

This is very different from listening and speaking, which are skills that are naturally developed. A developing fetus without auditory deficits begins listening to sounds around them before birth and the process continues throughout their lives. Exposure and experience are required, of course, but babies come into the world with the tools they need for listening and speaking. Well before infants can understand any words, they find speech interesting to listen to and prefer it to other kinds of sounds (Shultz & Vouloumanos, 2010).

An individual who speaks and understands English, but lacks the skill to read it, is considered to be functionally illiterate. Have you ever encountered someone who is extremely intelligent and witty, but lacks the ability to read? Those individuals function by having someone else who reads information on their behalf for clarification. Or the same individual with the reading deficit will have to be taught how to read whatever formal language is required in the country where they live, in order to fully transact their affairs independently.

Contrary to listening, reading is a skill that must be learned. Individuals must be taught how to read. Children who do not know how to read, for example, are not drawn to look at writing in the same way that babies who cannot understand spoken words are drawn to listen to speech (Evans & Saint-Aubin, 2005). We must remember that prehistoric people spoke languages that didn't have any formal scripts for many thousands of years before the introduction of the first scripted language. The cuneiform script, created in Mesopotamia, present-day Iraq, ca. 3200 BC, was the first scripted language. It was used for business transaction purposes (counting and recording). It is also the only writing system which can be traced to its earliest prehistoric origin.

Few of those prehistoric people had the idea that one could symbolize abstract units of language with visible marks. It's unrealistic to expect young children to discover such an advanced skill of reading without explicitly providing the necessary instruction. People are as good as their environments and experiences. We must give children today the same length of time it took their ancestors to invent and learn their writing system. Written language is learned rather differently than spoken language. Thus, it is not realistic to expect children to learn very much about how their writing system works from being exposed to print while being read to. The whole-language concept has derailed the importance of direct instruction which must also be present to ensure that children learn the mechanics of letter-sound relationships in order to become proficient readers.

Words to the Educator Who Teaches Reading

The strategies for teaching phonics presented in this chapter have been tested and yielded much success in my classroom with both typically developing and atypically developing (Special Education) students. They are not meant to relinquish the adult of their responsibility to be creative and make the necessary adjustments based on student's needs, personal preferences, and best practices. These suggestions are meant to empower the adults working with students by providing practical ideas and strategies from practitioners to bolter existing practices, or to be used as a foundation that one can build upon at home or at school.

My first suggestion for you, as a teacher, is to emotionally connect with the student. If that means you learn how to say "*hello*" in their native languages (English learners) or "*I'm happy to have you here*", you would be making a meaningful impact on that student and he/ she will be more willing to learn from you because relationships are very important. Better yet, include a word from the skill you are working on in your greeting in the language the student speaks. For this example, a student who does not speak English was referenced, but truthfully this holds true for students of all backgrounds. Every student must feel like they are an important part of your classroom or home learning environment.

Instructional practices should be driven by students learning needs and their abilities. Differentiation is one of the most frequently-used words in the education field, as it relates to addressing students' needs based on their abilities. If you are an educator, then you've surely heard a plethora of definitions for this word and seen several examples of what it should look like. You probably even have your own definition for and instructional methods for differentiation. Rely on that knowledge to create stimulating and engaging environments that meet their needs when based on varying paces, learning styles, and prior experience with topics.

Having taught grades (k-5) for years, I've concluded that the teacher plays a huge role in the success of the students, especially early learners. I am not negating the very important role that the home plays, because parents and caregivers are their child's first teachers. All of my years of teaching experiences were in the inner city or with kids from marginalized populations. I have also taught internationally and was placed with similar populations, but it was even more challenging, because there was a language barrier. During this experience, I had both absent parents and the ones who showed up frustrated because wanted to their child to earn only A's but they couldn't support their children learning at home. In addition to all of that, I needed a translator to communicate them. So please believe me when I say, I understand the challenges.

An important part of improving children's reading performance is improving the teacher's training on how to provide effective reading instruction. The assumption that every teacher knows how to teach their students to read is FALSE! It is very important that teachers and parents are well-equipped with the knowledge required to teach reading properly and that they have access

to support materials that will empower them to deliver quality instruction to their students.

Words to the Parent Who Teaches Reading

The strategies and content in this book can also be used for parents who are struggling to teach their children how to read and write. Parents, your child is never too young to begin learning. In fact, the moment a baby enters this physical world, learning begins, so it is very important that you are selective, intentional, and strategic about what they learn and how they learn it.

A good place to begin formal reading education is with this book and the many other resources available online. Young children primarily learn through play. So, spending time playing with your child with letters and speaking clearly to them is one of the most valuable investments you can make as a parent or guardian. If you believe that you just aren't cut out to be a teacher, join the list of folks attending "YouTube® University". Pull up videos on teaching your child the English alphabet (most of them will be teaching both the letters and their sounds). Engage in the activities on the video with your child.

Word Classifications

In this chapter, words will be classified by three colors: red, yellow, and green. Table 2.1 provides examples of each. Red words are usually nonsense words which are made up by randomly combining vowels and consonants. Creating red words, or nonsense words, should be encouraged, especially by early learners, and reinforced by providing an actual word – a green word- with the same number of letter from the student's example. Green words are words that are compliant to the phonetic rules and follow one or more of the spelling patterns. These words consist of digraphs, open, close syllables, silent -e, and any of the many phonic rules which you will learn about later in this chapter. Green words are decodable words. Yellow words are those words that defy phonetic rules and cannot be sounded out because they don't follow any spelling pattern. They are yellow, because they need to be approached with caution and require more thinking. These are also called "sight words" because they need to be memorized, to avoid the unnecessary effort of attempting to decode them.

Next in the discussion, come the types of syllables, which are the same as the types of spelling patterns. It is recommended that the first three syllable patterns be introduced at the end of first grade and are reinforced or built upon during the student's entire school career through twelfth grade. The fourth and fifth syllable patterns are recommended to be introduced at the end of third grade and reinforced or built upon through twelfth grade. Finally, it is recommended that the sixth syllable pattern be taught from fourth grade through twelfth grade. In order for children to become good readers they must be taught phonemic awareness, then phonics, and then fluency.

Table 2.1 Examples of Red, Yellow, and Green Words

Red (Nonsense) Words				
md	caf	suv	rad	pof
Green (Decodable) Words				
make	drink	stove	home	money
Yellow (Sight) Words				
must	new	into	are	ate
now	this	them	there	those
mis-	wrong	misfire	3%	

Figure 2.1 Terms and Definition Related to Phonics

Phonemic awareness- Phonemic awareness skills-the ability to manipulate the sounds that make up spoken language
Phonic skills- Phonic Skills-the understanding that there are relationships between letters and sounds
Fluency skills- Fluency skills-reading with accuracy, speed, and expression; and the application of reading comprehension strategies to enhance understanding and enjoyment of what they read.

Extensive research has shown that systematic phonics instruction leads to better acquisition of words than whole-language instruction does. Psychological science has provided evidence for the value and importance of deliberate phonics instruction. Unlike whole-language instruction, which is an innate trait every person possesses (language acquisition), letter and sounds relationships and determining how they relate is not automatically acquired by individuals, it must be taught. Research data, best practices, and personal experiences have been used to give a clear picture of what is needed to help children be successful in reading, starting with the phonics skills listed in Table 2.2. Each of these skills will be explored in more detail throughout this chapter.

Table 2.2 Phonics Skills Sequence Table

Order of Sequence	Skill (Letter Combination)	Description of Skill
1	Consonant Vowel/Vowel Consonant (VC/VC)	When two letters combine to make a word.
2	Consonant Vowel Consonant (CVC)	When a combination of three letters to from a word.
3	Long Vowel spelling patterns (CVC*E*)	This pattern creates the "magic" or silent *e* and other long vowel spelling patterns.
4	Beginning and Ending Consonant Blends	When two consonants combine to make one sound in which both letters are heard.
5	Consonant Diagraph	When two consonants combine to make one sound that can be at the beginning or end of a word.
6	Decoding / Syllabication / Spelling Patterns	This is the use of letter-sound relationship to correctly pronounce words and understand how words are broken into syllables. These are spelling patterns where the vowel sounds are declared open, closed, or the word follows the silent or magic *E* rule, but at this point there are usually more than three or four letters in the word.
7	Vowels Diphthongs	This is a sound formed by combining two vowels into a single syllable.
8	R-controlled syllable sounds	In these words, you hear the R sound louder than the vowel they come before or after.
9	Consonant LE suffix	L combined with the letter E at the end of a word, but usually hear only the L sound and the E is silent.
10	Double consonant	This happens when two consonant are together in a word and the two letters sound as one.
11	Advance Syllabication Patterns VCCV, VCV, & VCCCV	This happens in words with three or more syllables. Use either of these multi-syllable patterns in decoding and pronouncing the word.

Phonics Skill #1: CV (Consonant Vowel) and VC (Vowel Consonant) Spelling Patterns

By now the assumption is that your students understand that vowels have long and short sounds and that they know all the consonant letter sounds. First, you should begin teaching the students how to combine a single consonant and vowel (CV) to make words like so, to, go, lo, do, no, me, he, and hi. Notice that in the consonant vowel patterns the vowels make the long sound, meaning, you can hear the letter's name.

Next, are the vowel consonant (VC) pattern words such as an, am, it, in, up, us, and on. Notice that in the vowel consonant pattern, the vowel is short, meaning, that it makes the letter's sound and you do not hear the letter's names.

These consonant–vowel and vowel-consonant patterns are recommended to be taught, at least, for the first twenty minutes of the ELA block for two weeks, providing ample time for students to practice. Incorporate videos or other props to make it more interactive and engaging for the students. Another strategy is to have two sets of students come to the front of the room and act out the letters while reading the words. This gives the students a more visual understanding of how the vowel is represented in each of the spelling patterns. Practice with red words is highly encouraged during this phase of learning phonics.

Phonics Skill #2: CVC Spelling Pattern

The next spelling pattern is the 3-letter, CVC (consonant-vowel-consonant) pattern. In the CVC pattern, the vowels in those words make the short vowel sound. Use the knowledge acquired from the previous lessons, have students begin to build new words by adding a vowel in the middle of each word family. Examples include man, can, jet, pit, hot, and cup. More examples can be found in Figure 2.2 It is also okay to make up some nonsense words as the goal here is not to read fluently as much as it is to practice decoding the sounds and forming words. You can help students practice this by modeling the mouth movements required to make the appropriate sounds. Table 2.3 contains some ideas for activities to use for teaching this concept.

Figure 2.2 CVC Spelling Example

man	pet	tip	dot	mud

Figure 2.3 Activities for Teaching Phonics Skill #2: CVC Spelling Pattern

☐ Make vowel tents by folding index cards in half.
☐ Make vowel houses using Styrofoam cups
☐ Use dried beans and a plat to allow children to write the letter sounds they hear in the words being spoken by the teacher. Other options for sensory are colored sand, raw rice, buttons, or clay

Instruction of this skill can be differentiated using stations.

After engaging in these activities, it is suggested that the next 10 minutes are used for spiral review the skill before moving on with instruction.

Phonics Skills #3 Long Vowel Spelling Patterns (*E* and other long vowel spelling patterns)

The first rule for spelling "long" vowels is the magic ** E** or Silent E rule. Whenever there are four letters in a word, the vowel in between the two consonants becomes long, (the letter says its name) by adding an "E" at the end of the word. Begin teaching this skill by using the CVC word families that students have already learned and add an "e" to the end of those words, making a new word. Remember that the final "e", "silent "e", or magic "e" changes the vowel sound from the short vowel sound to the long vowel sound. Some examples are below:

- man +e = mane
- can + e = cane
- fam + e = fame
- bit + e = bite

These are only suggestions. Use your creativity and knowledge of your students to make this exercise more relevant to your own instruction.

The Vowel Team or Vowel Digraph Rule

This rules states that when two vowels are together, only one makes a sound (usually the first vowel) and the other is silent. This means that the vowel duo only makes one long vowel sound, which is what is seen in the tables for each long vowel spelling. You can help your students to remember this by using this analogy: when two vowels go walking, the first vowel acts as the parent and says its name and the second vowel is the baby who hasn't learned to speak— one vowel does the talking and the other is silent. Although there are times when the rule changes, this is the case most times especially in beginner's vocabulary.

Table 2.3 Long Vowel Spelling Patterns (*E* and other long vowel spellings)

Consonant-Vowel-Consonant-E or silent "E"				
*a*e**	*e*e**	*i*e***	*o*e**	*u*e**
cak*e*	Pet*e*	pik*e*	tot*e*	tun*e*
Long "A" – ai, ay, a**e** (magic or silent E), or eigh				
ai	ay	a**e**	eigh	
braid	away	make	eight	
Long "E" = ee, ey, and ea (**NOTE**: ee in the middle or at the end of a word makes the long "E" sound.) (**NOTE**: ea makes three sounds: read, bread – the short E, and steak – the long A)				
ee	ey	ea		
need	key	teach		
Long "I" = igh, ie, and i**e** (magic or silent E)				
igh	ie	i**w**		
high	pie	pike		
Long "O" = oa, oe, ow, and o**e** (**NOTE**: ow makes two sounds snow-long O and plow-as in owl)				
oa	oe	ow	o**e**	
boat	toe	snow	bore	
Long "U" =ui, eu, ue, and u**e** (silent or magic E)				
ui	eu	ue	u**e**	
fruit	feud	endue	cube	

Phonics Skill #4: Beginning and Ending Consonant Blends Pattern

Beginning consonant blends happens when two or more consonants are together at the beginning of a word and each letter sound is heard in the blend. The most common beginning consonant blends include: bl, br, cl, cr, dr, fr, tr, fl, gl, gr, pl, pr, sl, sm, sp st, dw, sw, tw, thr, shr, spr, scr, and str.

Table 2.4. Beginning Consonant Blends Examples

br	gr	fr	cl	fl	pl	str	thr	spl
brag	grid	frog	clap	flop	plead	strip	throw	split
brit	grill	frail	clam	fled	plum	strange	thread	splash

Consonant blends can also occur at the end of words and include: ct, ft, lt, xt, pt, st, lp, il, if, id, nd, sk, sp, ld, and mp. The combined consonant letters at the end of the word are called ending consonant blends. With the knowledge of what a beginning consonant blend is, the same understanding applies to ending blends – each letter sound is heard in the blend.

Table 2.5 Ending Consonant Blends Examples

mp	nd	nk	ft	st	ld	xt	lf
pump	hand	thank	left	must	held	next	self
jump	blend	skunk	craft	rust	weld	text	shelf

These examples have not nearly exhausted the number of beginning and ending blends. As the students' phonics skills improve, they should notice that blends the "sc" and "sk" can be used at both the beginning and ending of words. "SK" in particular, tends to be an ending blend. Regardless of where it shows up in a word, the blend makes the exact same sound.

Remember while practicing each skill, include nonsense words, it is perfectly fine for young learners. Although our intended outcome is ensuring that students are confident with the skills we are teaching, we also know that children can learn a lot through PLAY! So the more playful and relaxed your teaching approach is with exploring the content, the more willing and engaged the students will be. Some activities are detailed in Figures 2.4 and 2.5

Figure 2.4 The Blending Bridge Activity

☐ Buy a booklet of construction paper, roll of yarn, and clothes pins from the dollar store
☐ Have the student choose their two favorite colors from the construction paper booklet.
☐ Use one color construction paper, cut it into four equal parts, and write several blends (both beginning and ending).
☐ Cut the other color construction paper into four equal parts and write four letters on each
Examples: andy, ook, oate, ooke, etc.
☐ Cut a 5-foot piece of yarn and tie, glue, or tape it from one end of a wall to the next
☐ Take any one of the blends cards and pin it to the beginning of the bridge (the line created with yarn).
☐ Than take as many of the other combination cards and clip 3 letter combination cards for each blend.
☐ Repeat same process for the other beginning blend cards (do this for at least five beginning blends).
☐ As an extension activity, complete the same steps for the ending blends.
☐ This time the other letter cards will begin the bridge and the ending digraph will be found at the end.
☐ Have the students read and record the all of the words they made.

Figure 2.5 Teaching Blending Skills Activity

Explicit instruction performed by the teacher:
☐ List the blends you will be teaching on the board.
☐ Show the students a consonant blend video (you can use YouTube, Flocabulary, or any other resource).
☐ Have your students tell you what blends they identified from the video (add some sort of reward).
☐ Have your students list the words they heard in the video.
☐ Ask the students if they know any words that rhyme with the words they listed.
☐ Categorize the words according to their beginning or consonant endings (whichever you are emphasizing in the lesson).

Phonics Skill #5: Consonant Digraph

Consonant digraphs are two letters combined to make one sound. Many times, the pair produces a unique sound that neither letter would produce on its own. The difference between blends and digraphs is that blends are two or three letters that make one sound representing all of the letters in the blend, and digraphs make one sound. Unlike the beginning and ending blends which usually keep their positions in words, the digraphs can be used at both the beginning and ending of words and still make the same sound. There is only one exception, the digraph "WH", which is a beginning sound only. It does not appear at the end of any English words.

The five most common digraphs are TH, WH, CH, SH, and PH (which makes the "F" sound). These consonants combined make a single phonetic sound and are read as one unit. There is an exception when working with the TH digraph. TH makes two sounds (hard and soft). The hard sound is heard in *thumb* and *three*. The soft TH sound is what you hear in the words *the, thee, them*, etc. There are many videos that can be used to help teach the digraph sound and skill.

Teaching this skill can be a bit mundane so teachers need to find ways to make instruction more interesting. A few of my favorite activities are highlighted in Figure 2.6.

Figure 2.6 Tips to Enhance Phonics Skills Instruction

☐ Use BrainPop videos
☐ Allow students to play online games
☐ Make up games using resources found in your classroom or the house
☐ Choose activities based on students' interests
☐ Use any activity that requires hand movements
☐ Give groups of students two colors of play dough. Say a word and then as a group, students determine which digraph they heard and use their play dough to shape out the digraph.
☐ Use songs, dancing and other manipulatives
☐ Conduct a Google® search for activities and worksheets

Table 2.6 Consonant Digraph Examples

Diagraphs	Words with beginning digraphs	Words with ending digraphs
TH	thump, thorn, throne, that	tooth, Ruth, mouth, with
WH	which, what, whip, when	No words
SH	shop, shoes, sheep, shame	rush, crush, brush, flush
CH	cheese, chest, Charles, chief	which, sandwich, watch, catch
PH	phonics, photo, Phillip, phrase	humph, photograph, staph, triumph

Figure 2.7 Flexing with Consonant Digraphs Activity

☐ Create consonant digraph letter cards for *sh, ch, wh, th,* (*ph* for grades 3 +) and instruct the students to add any three letters **after** each digraph, building a new word for each.
☐ Have the students read and record the new beginning digraph words on a separate sheet of paper.
☐ Have the students put three or more letters **before** each digraph and create three new words for each.
☐ Have the students read and record these ending digraph words on separate sheet of paper.
☐ On another sheet of paper, create a chart with eight or ten columns (depending on the student's grade level) and label the columns according to the digraphs.
☐ Have the students cut out all of the words they created from both exercises and glue each word in its appropriate column of the chart depending on the beginning or ending diagraph.

Depending on the grade and age of the child, each of the skills previously mentioned skills should be taught within 20 weeks, on average. This will allow students time to gain a full understanding of the concepts and sufficient time to practice, which will lead to a faster acquisition of the more complex skills.

Phonics Skills #6: Decoding /Syllabication

Decoding/syllabication is such a vast and ever-evolving topic. Providing a strong foundation for young learners will provide a means for the more complex skills to be easily assessed in the future. Remember, the purpose of the chapter to provide some tips for teachers and parents which will help them empower their students and children to develop a love for learning so they can become successful readers. Frankly, the process of perfecting reading skills is an ongoing process. Every day we read and interact with materials that are new to us. Sometime we read something and have to step back and reread it just to be able to make sense of it or even be able to apply it to our lives. This is why syllabication or decoding is so important.

What are Syllables?

A syllable is a unit of pronunciation having one vowel sound. It may, or may not, include a consonant or have a means by which a word can be separated. Syllables are used to form the whole or a part of a word. For example, look at the word "*mother*" there are two syllables in "*mother*": mo + ther. In mother, you hear two short vowels sounds: they are the short O and short E sounds.

The word "*friends*" has a total of 7 letters, but only has one syllable. By definition, a syllable is a unit of a word with one vowel sound, which may or may not have a consonant as part of the sound or a means by which the word can be separated. In the word "*friend*" there is only 1 vowel sound, although there are 2 vowels in the word. This is a perfect example of vowel teams' rule (when 2 vowels go walking, only one does the talking). Technically, all of your previous lessons up to this point have been on syllables. At this point, syllables are now being stressed, because the children should be ready to manipulate more letters in their words and speaking and it's important that they learn how to use the rules for decoding. Figure 2.8 provides a quick reference of the characteristics of syllables.

Figure 2.8 Characteristics of Syllables

☐ a syllable can be only one letter if it's a vowel (o, a, i)
☐ a syllable can be one small word, as in your VC and CV, and CVC pattern words (in, on, cup, tap)
☐ words that have many vowels tend to have many syllables (par/tak/ers)
☐ the letter "U" does not count as a syllable if it comes after the letter "Q" (qu/een, quack, quar/ter)
☐ longer words usually have two or more syllables

What decoding?

Decoding is the ability to apply your knowledge of letter-sound relationships, including knowledge of letter patterns, to correctly pronounce written words. Understanding these relationships gives children the ability to recognize familiar words quickly and to figure out unfamiliar words.

What is Syllabication?

Syllabication is a specific strategy used to help young learners become a more accurate reader. By breaking a word into small, manageable syllables, identifying the vowel sounds within each syllable, and sounding out a word syllable by syllable, the reader learns the process of syllabication step by step. This process teaches students how to see parts of a word, hear the individual sounds, and then read the word.

At this point, reading instruction should build on the students' strength with 3- and 4- or more letter words. Instruction should also be intentional towards making sure the longer words that are being introduced, are words that are relevant to the children's lives. This is a good time to use words of their favorite items around the house or classroom. Also, try to select words that have at least 2 or 3 syllables. Table 2.7 lists example of word expansion and syllabication.

Table 2.7 Examples of Expanded Words and Syllabication

Detached Syllables (1 syllable)	Suggested Word (more than 1 syllable)
man	manuel = 3 syllables = man + u +el
van	vanish = 2 syllables = van+ ish
dem	democrat = 3 syllables = dem + o + crat
dan	daniel =2 syllables = dan + iel
fam	family = 3 syllables = fam + i +ly
hun	hun = 2 syllables = hunt + er
hot	hotter = 2 syllables = hot +ter
din	dinner = 2 syllables = din + ner

Words with Closed Syllables (CVC Syllabication)

These syllables are divided at the closed vowel sound. Closed syllable words are words that have a vowel sound "closed in" between consonants. See the examples in Figure 2.9.

Figure 2.9 Examples of Words with Closed Syllables

sun/set	bas/ket	mit/ten	muf/fin	cab/in

Words with Open Syllables (CVCV Syllabication)

These syllables are divided at the open vowel sound. Open syllable words are words that have an open vowel sound in the beginning, middle, and ends with a long vowel sound. See the examples in Figure 2.10.

Figure 2.10 Examples of Words with Open Syllables

la/dy	tru/ly	ro/de/o	cra/zy	emp/ty

Phonics Skills #7: Vowel Diphthong Syllable

A diphthong is a sound formed by combining two vowels into a single syllable. The two most common diphthongs in the English language are the letters combinations "oy"/"oi", as in "boy" or "coin", and "ow"/ "ou", as in "cloud" or "cow". Other vowel diphthongs are: ai, ay, igh, ee, etc. In short, a vowel diphthong is just another name for the vowel teams (although there is more than one vowel, only one sound is heard).

This skill can be practiced by having the students call out vowel teams or diphthongs while you write them out on the board. Then, encourage them to say any word that comes to their minds using the diphthongs (freestyle and play with nonsense words). Some examples of red (nonsense) and green words that can be created with vowel diphthongs are listed in Table 2.8.

Table 2.8 Red and Green Words Created Using Vowel Diphthong

Green Words				
"AW"/ "AU"	"OY"/ "OI"	"OW"/"OU"		
straw, law, saw	toy, boy, hoy	cow, mow, now		
cause, haul, author	oil, coin, noise	cloud, house, loud		
Red (nonsense words)				
ney	choi	tei	toid	smau

Table 2.9 contains words consisting of open, closed, silent-e and diphthong syllables. Have your students read the words and determine which syllable pattern and diphthong are used in each word.

Table 2.9 Combined types of Syllables Example

in/stead (closed)	ig/loo (open)	trea/son (closed)	mai/den (closed)	en./joy (open)
cof/fee (open)	an/noy (open)	free/ly (open)	fol/low (closed)	heav/y (open)

Phonics Skills #8: R-Controlled Syllables: ar, er, ir, or, and ur

R-controlled syllables exist in words where the vowel sound is neither long nor short. The vowel sound is controlled by the letter "R" and the /r/ sound. The vowel before the R does not make its regular long or short sound. Some rules for R-controlled syllables are listed in Figure 2.11.

Figure 2.11 Rules of R-Controlled Syllables

☐ "ar" says /ar/ as in far
☐ "ar" can also say /er/ like in the word holler (if the ar doesn't have an accent)
☐ "or" says /or/ as in dork or fork
☐ "or" after w says /er/ as in work
☐ if "or" is used at the end of a word without the accent it makes the /er/ sound like doctor and advisor

R-controlled syllables can be practiced using nonsense words. This helps children strengthen their understanding of the r-controlled syllables, so that they are able to easily identify and read words that contain r-controlled syllables. This skill can be practiced as both during the "Do-Now" or it can be embedded into the actual instruction.

Figure 2.12 Nonsense R-controlled Words

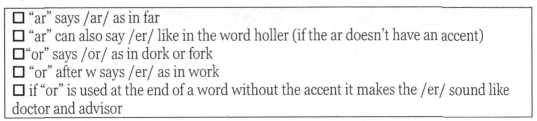

ber	hort	worp	tharp	cler

A suggested activity for practicing this skill is to have a student choose a word from a table of words, read it, and then say which syllable pattern they recognize in the word (r-controlled, open, closed, silent-e, diphthong). This is called the melting pot strategy and twenty sample words that can be used are listed in Figure 2.13.

Figure 2.13 Sample Melting Pot Strategy Words

1. la/bor	11. thirst/y
2. car/pool	12. star/light
3. sup/per	13. tu/mor
4. riv/er	14. so/lar
5. me/ter	15. sur/prise
6. tur/bine	16. bea/ver

Phonics Skills #9: Consonant-LE / Vowel Consonant Syllables (Grades 4-12)

Consonant –le is a syllable that only appears at the end of a word. The final e is silent. Only the two preceding consonants are heard. When looking in the dictionary, these syllables will be shown like this: b'l, d'l, f'l, etc. Examples are listed in Table 2.10. The consonant at the beginning of the syllable determines its sound that is made.

Table 2.10 Consonant -le Examples

Consonant –le Syllable	Example Words			
ble	bubble	rumble	table	stable
dle	bundle	candle	handle	puddle
fle	baffle	rifle	rattle	ruffle
gle	bugle	gargle	giggle	jungle
kle	buckle	ankle	fickle	pickle
ple	apple	dimple	ripple	sample
tle	battle	bottle	cattle	little
zle	puzzle	razzle	dazzle	sizzle
Stle	nestle	trestle	wrestle	hustle

Suffix Use Phonics

A suffix is a word ending that is added to a word that changes the meaning of the word. Most of the suffixes we use in our words today originated from Latin (a collection of Italic languages), French, and Greek. Just as numerous as the origin of suffixes is the number of suffixes that exist. For the purpose of making the instruction relevant, this chapter will focus on the most commonly used suffixes. Table 2.11 highlights some of the most common suffixes and the grade levels in which students are most likely to encounter them frequently.

Because the suffix is added to a word and changes the meaning of the word, we must also learn what the word before adding the suffix is called. A word without a suffix added to it is called a base word or root word. Play (base word) + -ed (suffix) = played, the past tense of play. The suffix --ed means the action is in the past or has already happened.

Table 2.11 Common Suffixes by Grade Level

Suffixes that begin with vowels	Suffixes that begin with consonant
ed, ing	ful ly
y er	less ness
est ist	ment
ish able	
Suggested Grade Levels to Teach Suffixes	
Grades 1 through 3 teach	-ed, -ing, -er, -y, -en, -est, -able, - ful, -less, -ness, -ment, - ly
Grades 4 and 5	-al, -ey, -ible, -ist, - ive, -ize, -ship, -ty, -ward
Grades 6 through 12	-ant, -ent, -ance, -ence, -ous, -ary, -ery, -ory, -ard, -dom, -hood

Each suffix has a meaning which is why when it is added to a word, it changes the meaning of the word. For example, the suffix *-less* means without. So the word hopeless means without hope. While the suffix *-ful* means full of, so we can change the meaning of the word hopeless by dropping the suffix *-less* and adding the suffix *–ful*. Now, the new word hope+ ful means full of hope.

Figure 2.14 The "LY" (Shouting E) Suffix Activity

> ☐ Create one-syllable words on card stock printer paper. (Another option would be magnetic letters from the dollar store).
> ☐ Place "LY" at the end or to the right of the table of your work area and then get the rest of the alphabet cards or magnetic letters.
> ☐ Take turns placing the letters to the left of the open syllable "LY" and have the child sound out the newly formed words. (Remember nonsense words are perfectly okay too.)
> ☐ After many rounds of the single letter, introduce letter combinations with "LY" then double the letters on the left to create blends, beginning digraph, and CVC (closed syllable) words, and have the child practice reading the newly formed words.
>
> Examples: bad + "LY"= badly;   sad +"LY"= sadly;   br (blend) + ight (long I spelling) + "LY"= brightly.

Phonic Skills#10: Double Consonant

Starting in second grade, students should be ready to learn the double consonant rule. This rule should be taught after the teacher or parent is confident that the child knows:

- what suffixes are
- that some suffixes begin with vowels and some begin with consonants
- the difference between one-and two-syllable words

Seize this opportunity to assess the student's retention of the concepts of syllables and decoding that were taught previously. Use the words in Table 2.12 to assess student proficiency. In this exercise the students are only looking for 1- or 2-syllable words as the doubling rule only works for words with 1- or 2-syllables.

Table 2.12 One & Two Syllable Words Review

Check the student's accuracy in identifying the number of syllables and determining if the syllables are open or closed.				
swim	fresh	porch	scrape	mustard
tender	shine	pencil	book	campus

The Doubling 1-1-1 Rule

The double consonant is when consonants appear together in a word, like ll, zz, ss, and pp; and the consonants are read as one sound, such as in words such as apple, bubble, carrot, puddle, and ruffle. The doubling rule applies to 1-syllable words and is called The 1-1-1 Doubling Rule. This is because it involves a 1-syllable word that ends in 1 consonant with 1 vowel before the final consonant. Table 2.13 explains it all in steps for following the rule and example of words formed after the rule has been applied.

Table 2.13 The 1-1-1 Doubling Rule Steps and Examples

When applying the 1-1-1 Doubling Rule...		
☐ If a 1-syllable base word ends with one consonant and a vowel before it, you must double the final consonant of the base word when adding a suffix that begins with a vowel.		
☐ If the base word ends with a consonant and the suffix begins with a consonant, do not double the ending consonant, just add the suffix.		
☐ If the base word ends with a vowel, just add the suffix to the word.		
☐ **NEVER** double the final letters w, x, and y.		
Double Consonant One Syllable Word with Suffix		
mad +est =maddest	thin + ing= thinning	box +ing =boxing
mad + er = madder	thin + er= thinner	play + er =player
Mad + ly =madly	thin + ness = thinness	snow + ed= snowed
	thin +ly = thinly	hope + ful =hopeful
Examples of Double Consonant Two Syllable Words		
When a 2-syllable word has a short vowel sound before the middle consonant, double the consonant.		
dinner	cottage	patted
rubber	drizzle	coffee

The final Phonics Skills that will be discussed are advanced forms of syllabication and should be introduced and reinforced in fourth through twelfth grades. However, for younger learners, this can be taught as an enrichment activity during the summer or before students being their fourth-grade school year.

Phonic Skills Rule #11: Advanced Syllabication (Words with Several Syllables)

Follow the formula in this table for dividing words into syllables.
1. Underline all the sounded vowels and diphthongs. A single e's at the end of a word is usually silent; cross out silent *e's*.
2. Count the sounded vowels. This tells you how many syllables are in the word.
3. See if the word contains a familiar suffix such as *–er*, *-ing*, *-ful*, or *–tion*. If it does, this is a part of the word you already know how to pronounce.

4. Label all vowels and consonants, starting with the first vowel.
 	
    Examples: a n c e s t o r   j u v e n i l e   t r i p p i n g
        v c c v c c v c   c v c v c v c   v c c v c c

5. See which pattern the vowels and consonants make: VCCV, VCV, or VCCCV
5a. Whenever 2 consonants come together in a word, divide between them: VC/CV. Never divide blends. **Examples:**   c o n t e n t   a d m i r e   a t m o s p h e r e   v c / c v c c   v c / c v c   v c / c v c / c c v c

5b. When only 1 consonant comes between 2 vowels, divide after the 1st vowel: V/CV. This makes an open syllable and the vowel usually has a long sound.
 	
Examples: s i / l e n t (not sil/ent)   v a / c a / t I o n (not vac/a/tion)
        v / c v c c   v / c v / c v c
 	
Pronounce the word with an open syllable. If this does not make a word that sounds familiar, divide after the consonant: VC/V
 	
Examples: s i / l e n t (not sil/ent)   v a c a / t i o n (not vac/a/tion)
        v / c v c c   v / c v / c v c
 	
Pronounce the word with an open syllable.
If this does not make a word that sounds familiar, divide after the consonant: vc/ccv.
 	
Examples: l i m i t (not li/mit)   c a b/ i n   (not ca/bin)
        v c / c v   v c / v c

5c. When 3 consonants come together, divide after the 1st consonant: VC/CCV. If this does not make a word that sounds familiar, divide after the second consonant: VCC/CV Examples: c o m / p l e t e   (not comp/ lete)   p u m p / k i n   (not pum/pkin)   v c/ c c v c   v c c / c v c
6. If a vowel combination is reversed, divide between the vowels. Each vowel will then have a sound. Examples: v i / o / l e t   v i / o / l e n t   d i / a l   n e / o n   p e /   o / ny

Figure 2.15 Advanced Syllabification Activity

The purpose of this exercise is to get the student to break up the word by syllables and read it.

☐ Write a word out and don't read the word aloud to students.
☐ Look at the word and circle the vowel sounds.
☐ Underline the consonants BETWEEN the vowels (don't worry about the other consonants).
☐ Determine which syllable division rule (VC/CV, V/CV, VC/V, or V/V) applies. (Students may have to attempt to read the word to choose between V/CV and VC/V).
☐ Mark the syllables in the word accordingly.
☐ Read the word.

Conclusion

Researchers link the relationships between students' reading abilities and their cognitive skills, to their abilities to critically think and problem solve. Reading, however, has to be taught because it enhances cognitive skills, but isn't as inherent as the ability to think. With careful, intentional, and relevant instruction children can become successful readers. How well students understand phonics and how to manipulate letters and sounds and their relationships to words, can empower children to unleash their inner geniuses. Many students perform below their academic capabilities due to deficits in their reading skills. Sadly, teachers and parents are oftentimes ill-prepared to provide the level of support children need to overcome these barriers. Parents, caregivers, and teachers alike can work together to ensure that our students can read and are equipped to take on other advanced intellectual tasks by providing a solid foundation of phonics.

Figure 2.14 Additional Resources for Teaching Phonics

Title	URL	Description
Florida Center for Reading Research	https://fcrr.org/resources/resources_sca.html	For grade level reading center activities.
My Teaching Station	https://www.myteachingstation.com/et-word-family-workbook-for-kindergarten	for CV and CVC word pattern activities.
Kindergarten Mom	https://kindergartenmom.com/i-can-read-free-printables/et-word-family-printables/	For free printable materials.
Hubbard's Cupboard	http://www.hubbardscupboard.org/	Interactive video and short stories
Starfall	https://www.starfall.com/h/	games, video, and activities
ABC Mouse	https://www.abcmouse.com	Games, videos, and other activities
ABCYA	https://www.abcya.com/	games and interactive learning
Teacher Pay Teacher	https://www.teacherspayteachers.com/	worksheets and activities created educators

CHAPTER THREE

VOCABULARY

According to Marzano (2013), "Children's vocabulary knowledge is directly linked to their success in school" (p. 5). Vocabulary is one of the key components in learning to read and it is also critical to reading comprehension. Vocabulary refers to a child's knowledge of words and meanings of words. It is not only the dictionary meanings of words, but also according to Steven Stahl (2005), implies how that word fits into the world. The words children know impact how well they comprehend texts. Words represent knowledge, and when that knowledge is limited, children struggle with comprehension of texts.

Vocabulary is acquired two ways: incidentally and intentionally (Honig, Diamong, & Gutlohn, 2008). Incidental learning takes place through indirect exposure and intentional learning occurs through direct and explicit instruction. Incidental learning of vocabulary happens during conversations, Read-Alouds, and other oral experiences with language. Intentional learning of vocabulary is direct instruction planned for the specific purpose of children acquiring new word meanings. This chapter will provide strategies and resources for both incidental and intentional learning of vocabulary in a classroom, as well as in an at-home setting.

Approach to Teaching Vocabulary in the Classroom

Incidental Learning of Vocabulary

Vocabulary is not something children will master. It is not a single concept that can be measured by a single assessment. It is an ongoing process and skill that children are continuously developing. According to Cunningham and Stanovich (1998), "most vocabulary is acquired incidentally." Through incidental learning, children are exposed to words and given opportunities to acquire words through reading, conversations, and other multimedia platforms.

Reading

If vocabulary improvement is the goal, then every classroom needs to make reading a priority and focus. Teachers must set the expectation that extensive reading occurs frequently and consistently. If it is a priority, it should be evident in teachers' practices, the daily schedule, routines and procedures, classroom arrangement, and the reading materials that are made available to children. Each of these approaches will be discussed in detail.

Children's books contain very rich and colorful language, which makes Read-Alouds a great way for children to acquire new vocabulary. A read-aloud is an instructional practice consisting of reading a text aloud with variations in delivery such as tone, pitch, rhythm, pace, volume, questions, and explanations that produce a fluent and enjoyable experience. One of the most important benefits of teachers reading aloud is the conversation that takes place after reading the text. Children are able to use their existing knowledge to connect to the text and make the words in the text more meaningful so they can be integrated into their vocabulary.

Children can continue to gain meaning of unfamiliar words through meaningful and purposeful conversations with their peers as well as through the use of Think-Alouds. A Think-Aloud is a strategy that allows individuals to listen as a teacher or peer verbalizes their thoughts while reading a selection orally with the purpose being to model how proficient or skilled readers construct meaning from a text. The think-aloud usually consists of describing what they are doing to monitor their comprehension of the text.

In some schools, administrators create the daily schedules for teachers that dictate the number of minutes required for each subject area, lunch, enrichment classes and recess with little to no autonomy to deviate. In other schools, teachers are given the minimum amount of time required for each content area and are allowed the autonomy to create their daily schedules. With either option, the daily schedule should include multiple opportunities for children to hear fluent reading and to read independently. In order for children to become better readers, they need to practice reading with a variety of genres, which will provide exposure to a wider selection of vocabulary words. At the same time, when children encounter unfamiliar words, explicit instruction must occur (see intentional learning).

When setting classroom routines and procedures, reading needs to be at the forefront. What happens when children come in early? What happens when children finish assignments early? What happens during dismissal? What do children do when your lesson concludes five minutes before lunchtime? What about when an administrator or colleague walks in to speak with you or during a restroom break? How about when you are pulled away unexpectedly for a few minutes? These are real-life situations, so teachers have to establish routines and procedures that include independent reading.

Upon entering a classroom, it should be easy to determine if reading is a focus. Is there a dedicated reading area? Does reading appear to be fun? Teachers have the power to change children's outlooks on reading by arranging the classroom to include a reading area and making that area fun and inviting. Suggested items to include in the reading area would be cool and colorful seating, pillows, carpet, sheer curtains, or anything else that makes the area special and different as opposed to a punishment.

Reading should not be used as a punishment. Too many times when students misbehave or break a class/school rule, recess or enrichment classes are taken away and students are forced to stay in and read. This sends the message that reading is not enjoyable, boring, and equivalent to a punishment. In order for students to view reading in a positive manner, the teachers, administrators and other adults in the school must make reading a priority and positive experience.

In order for children to read extensively, they must be exposed to a variety of texts. As a classroom teacher, I was taught to organize my classroom libraries according to text complexity. Research now tells us that text should be organized by complexity *and* topic as opposed to complexity alone. According to Elfrieda H. Hiebert, a leading researcher in vocabulary development (2020), texts organized around complexity and topic "give children the chance to generalize their knowledge of words across texts and, in the process, build a coherent knowledge base – the foundation of proficient comprehension." In other words, children are able to associate words with a concept. This allows them to acquire more vocabulary words at the same time, instead of learning vocabulary words in isolation. For example, if a child reads several stories about baseball, they could potentially be exposed to words such as: baseball, uniform, umpire, deck, walk, stolen base, runs, champion, diamond, designated hitter, relief pitcher, etc. These words may not appear in a traditional reading program with the meanings they have as it relates to baseball. The children can learn far more words conceptually, than in isolation, because they have context which helps to anchor the new vocabulary.

Conversations

The experiences children have with oral language are critical to the incidental learning of vocabulary. Research by Cabell, Justice, McGinty, Decoster, & Forston, (2015), states that "Conversations have been shown to be a powerful means of supporting children's awareness and knowledge of vocabulary." In the classroom, teachers must organize their classrooms and lessons to include opportunities for children to engage in conversations with not only the teacher, but their peers as well. This section will contain several strategies that can be used to encourage students to engage in meaningful and purposeful conversations in the classroom to help build vocabulary.

Classrooms should be organized with children working collaboratively in flexible groups with multiple opportunities to talk. Strategies such as Think- Pair-Share, Turn and Talk or Partner Talk, are simple learning strategies in which children pair up and learn by discussing and then sharing their thoughts and ideas on the concept or idea being taught.

The Socratic Circle is a strategy where the teacher, like Socrates, claims to not know anything which forces the children into the role of the teacher. Using the Socratic Circle, the children are placed in two circles. One group conducts a student-led discussion around a specific text and/or question, while the other group watches the discussion and keeps track of the direction of the conversation. After a certain amount of time, the groups switch roles. The outside group must remain silent, but can reference statements made by the other group. The teacher's role is more of an observer, and steps into the conversation only to guide it in a particular direction.

A third strategy is to use a soft ball or other item that can be tossed to a child without the chance of an injury. After posing a question, toss the ball/item to a child to respond. Once the child responds, he/she will toss the ball/item to another child to respond. This will continue until the conversation runs its course or the teacher wants to pose a different question or change directions in the lesson. These strategies cause children to talk and to listen, thus providing them with opportunities to learn from their peers and acquire new vocabulary.

Multimedia Platforms

In the world we live in today, children are accustomed to using various forms of technology. They are comfortable using computers, tablets, and phones to quickly gather information. Educational companies are tapping into the children's interests and desires to use various forms of technology to learn. Websites and software are now available for children to access books, educational games, videos, video conferencing, and more. These various multimedia platforms all expose children to new vocabulary and methods to acquire that knowledge.

Table 3.1 Summary of Incidental Vocabulary Learning Strategies for the Classroom

Incidental Vocabulary Strategy	How to Implement the Strategy
Reading Strategies	
Prioritized Reading	☐ Numerous planned reading opportunities ☐ Daily routines for independent reading ☐ Create inviting reading area in classroom ☐ Reading materials varying by topic and complexity ☐ Avoid using reading as a punishment
Read-Alouds	☐ Vary tone, pitch, rhythm, pace, volume, questions, and explanations while reading texts aloud to students
Conversations	
Flexible Group Activities	☐ Think-Pair Share ☐ Turn and Talk ☐ Partner Talk
Socratic Circle	☐ Divide students into two groups ☐ One group discusses, while the other reserves ☐ Teacher observes ☐ Have groups exchange roles and repeat
Share Your Thoughts	☐ Teacher poses a question and tosses a ball to a student ☐ Student responds to question ☐ Student tosses ball to another student to respond to question ☐ Repeat
Technology-Based Platforms	
Multimedia Programs	☐ Access Books ☐ Educational Games ☐ Videos/Video Conferencing

Intentional Learning of Vocabulary

The vocabulary knowledge of children varies widely and the gap in knowledge begins before children enter school. In 1995, Hart and Risley found that three-year-olds from more affluent homes had oral vocabulary as much as five times larger than children from disadvantaged homes. The implication for this is that without intervention, the gap would continue to grow and actually widen as children proceed through school.

In order to close the vocabulary gap, "vocabulary acquisition must be accelerated (Biemiller, 2005b)." According to the National Reading Panel (2000), explicit/intentional instruction of vocabulary is highly effective and includes words and word-learning strategies. Although explicit/intentional instruction is highly effective, children only acquire about two words a day or 10 words a week (Biemiller, 2005b). In the most ambitious and aggressive vocabulary programs, there are more words to be learned than can be directly taught. Therefore, developing effective word-learning strategies is critical to reading and understanding unfamiliar words.

Word-learning Strategies

Word-learning strategies include dictionary use, morphological analysis, semantic connections, and contextual analysis. When providing intentional vocabulary instruction, teachers must decide what words they will explicitly teach. Beck, McKeown, and Kucan (2013) recommend that we select words that are used frequently and appear across a variety of genres and texts. These words are referred to as Tier Two words. These are words that tend to be unfamiliar, but students may encounter in their readings and would benefit from knowing the meaning. Tier One words are words that are used in our everyday speech and are usually familiar to most students. Tier Three words on the other hand, are words that appear less frequently and will only be encountered in specific subjects. For examples of tiered words, see Table 3.2.

When selecting words to explicitly teach, teachers should consider words that are important to understanding a specific reading selection or concept and words that are generally useful for children to know and are likely to encounter with some frequency in their reading. Many times multiple meaning words are critical to understanding the selection. Children may be familiar with the word in one context, but not another. For example, children may be familiar with the word *consumer* meaning "a person or thing that eats or uses something", but may not be familiar with it in social studies context, meaning "a person who purchases goods and services for personal use". The word *consumer* would need to be explicitly taught in order for children to understand the selection.

Table 3.2 Tiered Vocabulary Words

Tier 1	Tier 2	Tier 3
☐ High-frequency words that appear in everyday conversations in texts children have already read ☐ Rarely require explicit instruction for English-Language Learners or children with limited vocabulary knowledge	☐ Occur frequently in texts children are reading or will be reading ☐ Do not occur in everyday conversations ☐ Make good choices for explicit instruction	☐ Low-frequency words that appear in specific genres of text or particular subjects that children are reading ☐ Should be explained when they are encountered or as needed
Examples: please, little, ball, red, girl	Examples: equation, experiment, artistic, conclusion, theme	Examples: hyperbole, ligament, divisor, generation, pollution

Dictionary Use

As a child in elementary school, I can remember teachers giving us a list of new words each week, with the express purpose of defining the words for homework. After a couple of weeks, I did not remember the definitions of many of the words. The reason for that is a lack of connection. The words were random, maybe appeared once in a story, but had no other real connection to my previous knowledge. While there are disadvantages to using this strategy, using the dictionary also has some advantages. Dictionary use allows children to understand multiple-meaning words and then select the correct meaning based on context clues. In addition to the parts of speech, most dictionaries will provide a sentence using the word and as well as synonyms and antonyms. Using that information could aid children in acquiring more vocabulary words.

The key is for the teacher to be sure to help children to make connections to the words. This can be done by associating an image with the word, having a discussion and connecting the word to something in the child's previous knowledge, or attaching a movement to the word. The simple connections to the words will make using a dictionary to define words a much more effective strategy. The Collins Dictionary is a free online dictionary/thesaurus that provides child friendly definitions, a real person to pronounce the words, reference materials, and more information about the words. The Collins Dictionary will help children to make genuine connections.

Morphemic Analysis

A morpheme is the smallest unit of meaning in a language or a word-part clue. There are two types of morphemes. Free morphemes are word parts that can stand alone as words, whereas bound morphemes or affixes are word parts that cannot stand alone as words. The word help is a free morpheme and represents the smallest unit of the word. The words helpful, helps, or helpless all include a bound morpheme. The bound morphemes are *–ful*, *-s*, and *–less*. They cannot stand alone as words and must be attached to a free morpheme. The word help has one morpheme and the words helpful, helps and helpless each have two. Bound morphemes that come at the beginning of a word are called prefixes, whereas those that come at the end of words are called suffixes.

Intentional/explicit instruction with morphemes involves teaching children the meanings of word parts. According to Biemiller (2005a), children can derive meanings of words if they are familiar with the meanings of root words and affixes.

Root words are words that form other words. Having knowledge of root words can help with understanding related words.

Prefixes and Suffixes

Prefixes alter the meaning of the root words to which they are attached. Graves (2004) explains the importance and benefits of teaching prefixes:

1. there are a small number of prefixes
2. prefixes are easily identified because they are located at
3. the beginning of words
4. the spelling of prefixes tends to be consistent
5. prefixes usually have a clear meaning

Researchers White, Sowell, and Yanagihara (1989), identified 20 prefixes that make up 97 percent of all of the words with prefixes (*see Table* 3.3) that appear in school reading materials, and four prefixes (un-, re-, in-, and dis) account for 58 percent of all of the words with prefixes.

Like prefixes, suffixes alter the meaning of words, but are attached to the end of words. There are two types of suffixes: inflectional and derivational. Inflectional suffixes do not change the part of speech, but do change the form of the word. These include verb forms, plurals, and comparatives/superlatives such as *–s*, *–es*, *–ed*, and *–ing*. Derivational suffixes alter the meaning of root words. Examples are *–ful*, *–less*, *–ment*, and *–ness*. According to White, Sowell, & Yanagihara (1989), inflectional suffixes occur most frequently in school reading materials, while derivational suffixes appear in less than 25 percent of all words that contain suffixes. Although derivational suffixes appear less frequently, researchers find the explicit teaching of them to be beneficial (Edwards et al. 2004). The most frequently used suffixes can be found in Table 3.4.

While teaching prefixes and suffixes is an effective strategy for teaching vocabulary overall, there are several limitations and exceptions to the rules. White, Sowell, and Yanagihara (1989), point out that *-in* means both not and in, and many times children get confused with words such as *uncle* which does not have a prefix, but appears to have the prefix -*un*. Teaching prefixes and suffixes will help children to significantly increase their vocabulary, but does have limitations. The process below will assist children in using this strategy:

Table 3.3 The 20 Most Frequently Used Prefixes in School Reading Materials

Prefix	Meaning	Example	Percent
un-	not	unfriendly	26%
re-	again, back	redo, return	14%
in-, im-, il-, ir	not	injustice, impossible	11%
dis-	not, opposite of	disagree	7%
en-, em-	cause to	encode, embrace	4%
non-	not	nonsense	4%
in-, im-	in, on	inhabit, imprint	4%
over-	too much	overdo	3%
mis-	wrong	misfire	3%
sub-	under-	submarine	3%
pre-	before	prefix	3%
inter-	between	interact	3%
fore-	before	forecast	3%
de-	not, opposite	deactivate	2%
trans-	across	transport	2%
super-	above	superstar	1%
semi-	half	semicircle	1%
anti-	against	antiwar	1%
mid-	middle	midway	1%
under-	below	undersea	1%
trans-	across	transport	2%

Based on White, Sowell, and Yanagihara 1989 taken from *Teaching Reading Sourcebook* 2008.

Table 3.4 The 20 Most Frequently Used Suffixes

Prefix	Meaning	Example	Percent
-s, -es	more than one	books, boxes	31%
-ed	past tense verbs	hopped	20%
-ing	verb form/present participle	running	14%
-ly	characteristic of	quickly	7%
-er, -or	one who	worker, actor	4%
-ion, -tion, -ation, -ition	act, process	occasion, attraction	4%
-able, -ible	can be done	comfortable	2%
-al, -ial	having characteristics of	personal	1%
-y	characterized by	happy	1%
-ness	state of, condition of	kindness	1%
-ity, -ty	state of	infinity	1%
-ment	action or process	enjoyment	1%
-ic	having characteristics of	linguistic	1%
-ous, -eous, -ious	possessing the qualities of	joyous	1%
-en	made of	wooden	1%
-er	comparative	higher	1%
-ive, -ative, -itive	adjective form of a noun	plaintive	1%
-ful	full of	careful	1%
-less	without	fearless	1%
-est	comparative	biggest	1%
all others			7%

Based on White, Sowell, and Yanagihara 1989 taken from *Teaching Reading Sourcebook* 2008

Figure 3.1 Using Word-Part Clues for Teaching Unfamiliar Words

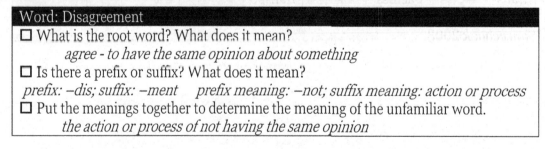

Word: Disagreement
☐ What is the root word? What does it mean?
agree - to have the same opinion about something
☐ Is there a prefix or suffix? What does it mean?
prefix: –dis; suffix: –ment   prefix meaning: –not; suffix meaning: action or process
☐ Put the meanings together to determine the meaning of the unfamiliar word.
the action or process of not having the same opinion

Greek and Latin roots are bound morphemes that must be attached to other morphemes and cannot stand alone. A small number of Greek and Latin roots are present in hundreds of thousands of words (Henry 2003). Words with Greek roots tend to be related to math and science, whereas Latin roots tend to have a more general-purpose meaning. Researchers Stahl and Nagy (2000) having differing opinions on the benefit of and how much time should be spent teaching Greek and Latin roots due to the exceptions and limitations. The common Greek and Latin roots in English are listed in Table 3.5.

Semantic Connections

Semantic connections refer to the connections between words as they relate to a specific concept. Word knowledge is developed in networks of words clustered into categories (Beck et al. 2002). Semantic mapping is tying one word or concept to other related words. The same model can be used to enhance vocabulary instruction with any reading program.

Table 3.5 Common Greek and Latin Roots in English

Root	Meaning	Origin	Example
astro	star	Greek	astronaut
aud	hear	Latin	audible
dict	say, tell	Latin	dictate
geo	earth	Greek	geology
graph	write, record	Greek	autograph
meter	measure	Greek	barometer
mit, miss	send	Latin	submit, mission
ology	study of	Greek	morphology
ped	foot	Latin	pedal
phon	sound	Greek	phonograph
port	carry	Latin	transport
spect	see	Latin	inspect
struct	build, form	Latin	construct
Tele	from afar	Greek	telephone

CORE Teaching Reading Sourcebook, 2008

To use this strategy, have children brainstorm words related to the concept. Write all words on the chart/map (see Table 3.6), then read the related text. After reading the text, have children to discuss the text and add any new words to the chart/map. The teacher should guide the discussion by having a series of questions that relate to the text and the concepts prepared. Children can work in small collaborative groups or complete the activity as a whole group. Once the questions are answered, have children work independently to select three to four words to use in sentences.

These questions can be used to guide the semantic mapping:

1. How are football and soccer the same?
2. How are they different?
3. Where are the different sports played?
4. Are all the sports played in stadiums?
5. Who oversees the games to make sure everyone follows the rules?
6. Name the different players for each sport.
7. Which sport would you prefer to play and why?

Another format of Semantic Mapping can be found in Figure 3.2. This format works the same with the main purpose being to have students to make connections between a word or phrase and other words or phrases. The words generated help to increase the students' vocabulary. Some of the questions that could be used to guide the discussion on transportation include:

1. Would you rather drive a car or ride a motorcycle?
2. Why?
3. Which mode of transportation would be the most interesting to
4. ride and why?
5. Which is the fastest mode of transportation?
6. Which is slowest?
7. Which is the most fun?

Figure 3.2 Transportation Semantic Map

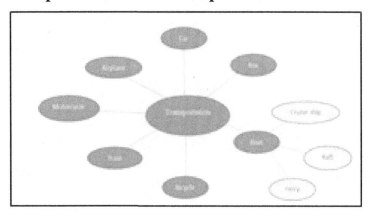

Word Maps

Word map graphic organizers help children visualize how words connect to each other and use their prior knowledge to make additional connections. Having children explore synonyms and antonyms is an effective way to enhance word knowledge. A synonym is a word with a similar meaning, and an antonym is a word with opposite or near opposite meaning. These graphic organizers can be completed as a whole group, small group, with a collaborative partner or independently during or after the reading process.

Figure 3.3 Synonyms Word Map

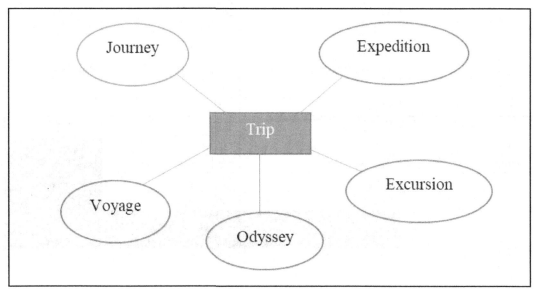

Figure 3.4 Antonyms Word Map

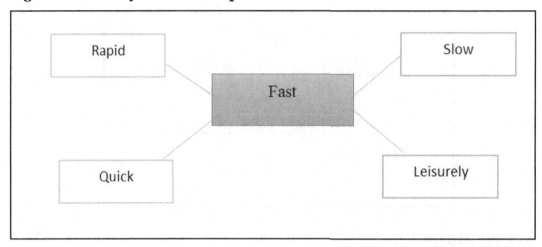

Table 3.6 Sample Semantic Map – SPORTS

Baseball	Basketball	Football	Soccer
Baseball	Basketball	Football	Soccer ball
Bat	Hoop	Pig skin	Goal
Bases	Net	Quarterback	Goalie
Homerun	Dribble	Downs	Referee
Umpire	Field goal	Yards/yard line	Goal line
Glove	Free throw	Kick off	Points
Diamond	Free throw line	Kick return	Extra time
Home plate	Three point shot	Punt	Penalty kick
Mound	Base line	Interception	Penalty
Base lines	Bench	Fumble	Block
Dug out	Tip off	Safety	Header
Bullpen	Rebound	Tackle	Throw in
Single	Jump ball	Catch	Save
Double	Travel/traveling	reception	Mid fielder
Triple	Turn over	Holding	Forward
Grand slam	Steal	Off sides	Defender
Hit	Block shot	Pass	Center
Strike out	Double dribble	Chains	
Pitch	Technical foul	Half time	
Pitcher	Referee	Quarter	
Foul ball	Over time	Over time	
Umpire			
Slide			

Word Banks or Word Walls

Word banks or word walls include displays of words that have been previously taught in order for children to reference, practice, and use the words as needed (O'Connor 2007). The words can be organized alphabetically or by similar patterns. Words with similar patterns or phonograms, such as could, would, and should might be introduced and taught together in sets. High frequency words are easier to reference in alphabetical order for younger children. Children can maintain personal journals or logs for their word banks.

Word walls (see Figure 3.5) are perfect for displaying semantic maps, concept charts, and word maps and should be present for every content area and concept taught. It is important for teachers to make the word wall a vital part of instruction, and integrate it into daily lessons. Having children recite the words, use them in their writings and oral responses, answer questions about the words, and categorize them are effective strategies that will make the word walls meaningful and effective. Teachers will need to be creative and intentional to make sure the word wall does not become unused wall décor.

Figure 3.5 Example of Word Wall

Table 3.7 Summary of Intentional Vocabulary Learning Strategies for the Classroom

Intentional Vocabulary Strategy	How to Implement the Strategy
Use Dictionary to Define Words	☐ Make connections to the words by associating an image with the word ☐ Have a discussion about the word connecting it to prior knowledge or attaching a movement to the word
Using Morphological Analysis (to Teach Meanings of Word Parts)	☐ Help students to identify and define base words and word parts that change the meanings of words. ☐ Teach prefixes and suffixes that occur most frequently in words. ☐ Teach students to use word-part clues to figure out unfamiliar words. ☐ Teach most common Greek and Latin roots.
Semantic Connections (Guide students in making connections between words as they relate to specific concepts.)	☐ Introduce and discuss a new concept. ☐ Have students brainstorm words they know related to the concept. ☐ Write words on a chart/map. ☐ Read related text, and then have students to discuss the text and add any new words to the chart/map. ☐ The teacher should have a series of questions prepared to guide the conversation.
Contextual Analysis (Guide students in analyzing/describing the words used in a text to determine their meanings as they relate to that specific text.)	☐ Teach students multiple meaning words and how to use context clues to determine the correct meaning. ☐ Teach synonyms and antonyms of words. ☐ Use word walls and word banks to keep track of new words learned and encourage students to reference and use words in the conversations and writings. ☐ Teach figurative language and idioms.

Table 3.8 Additional Ideas for Introducing & Teaching Vocabulary

Vocabulary Strategy	How to Implement the Strategy
Six-Step Vocabulary Sequence	☐ Notice and Name – Point out and refer to the word in context. Have the child say the word and discuss it (based on previous knowledge, if they have ever heard it before, or based on what they think it means, if they have not heard it before). ☐ Provide a child-friendly definition. (The Collins Dictionary online is a great tool to use here.) ☐ Construct a word web. (Refer to the section on Semantic Connections.) ☐ Provide and/or guide the child to provide additional examples and encourage personal connections. ☐ Add the word to the word wall. ☐ Have children to add it to their personal word banks.
Word Detective Game	☐ The teacher or leader would take the teacher made cards and ask questions related to the vocabulary words. This can be played whole or small group. **Example** – *I'm thinking of a word that means a long trip that was in our story. What is that word? Odyssey. This word can be either of the two words that described the main character as he walked to school. Slow or leisurely?*
I Have...Who Has?	☐ Create cards with a homophone on one side of the card and the definition of another homophone on the other side. ☐ On the next card, provide the answer to this and a new homophone. This can be played as a whole or small group. **Example:** Child 1 – *Who has a word that means the opposite of day?* Child 2 – *I have night. Who has the word that makes the leaves blow?* Child 3 – *I have wind. Who has...?*
Flap Books	☐ Either provide or allow the child to create a two- or three-page flip book. ☐ Have the children to write the word under the first flap, a child friendly definition under the second flap and a sketch or image that relates to the word under the third flap.

	FLAP BOOKS Things You Might Find on the Beach	Evidence of Humans	Evidence of Plants	Evidence of Animals
Figurative Language	☐ Have the child illustrate the literal and figurative meanings of idioms and other figurative language expressions in their vocabulary notebooks.
I Wonder Wall/Curiosity Corner	☐ Have a wall or area dedicated to researching and answering questions the children may have always wanted to know more about. (These may be totally unrelated to the current classroom topics and should take place when children have completed assignments, arrive early, during dismissal or at home.) ☐ Have the children should post the answers on the wall for others to learn from as well. (The motivation is for children to enhance their research and reading skills while pursuing their personal interest. The reading and writing will increase their vocabulary and overall knowledge.) **Example:** *I wonder what state in the United States does the sun shine first each day. Between January 11 and March 6 as well as between October 7 and November 29, the sun first hits the top of Cadillac Mountain on the island of Mt. Desert, Maine.*

Approach to Teaching Vocabulary at Home

Before a child can learn to read or improve comprehension skills, they need to have a well-rounded knowledge of words and their meanings. As a parent, having the desire to assist your child in improving reading skills and not having the knowledge to do so can be extremely frustrating. This section will provide you with effective strategies that are simple, easy to implement, and sure to help improve your child's knowledge of vocabulary.

Vocabulary is one of the key components in the reading process and is critical to reading comprehension. As stated in the previous section, I want to reiterate the importance of vocabulary and its impact on comprehension. Vocabulary refers to knowledge of words and word meanings. It is not only the dictionary meanings of words, but also according to Stahl (2005), implies how that word fits into the world. The words children know impact how well they comprehend texts. Words represent knowledge, and when that knowledge is limited, children struggle with comprehension of texts.

Vocabulary is acquired incidentally and intentionally (Honig, Diamong, & Gutlohn, 2008). Incidental learning takes place through indirect exposure and intentional learning occurs through direct and explicit instruction of specific words and word-learning strategies. Incidental learning happens during conversations, Read-Alouds and other oral language experiences. Intentional learning is direct instruction planned with the express purpose of children acquiring new word meanings.

Strategies for Teaching Vocabulary at Home

Conversations

Conversations have been shown to be one of the most powerful means of supporting the awareness and knowledge of vocabulary (Cabell, Justice, McGinty, DeCoster, & Fortson, 2015). As a parent, this strategy is very natural. Conversations happen organically every day. In order to make this strategy more powerful, parents can be intentional in exposing children to specific vocabulary words.

Read-Alouds

There are numerous benefits of reading to and with your child. According to the report *Becoming a Nation of Readers (1984)*, the single most important activity for building knowledge and leading to success in reading is reading aloud to children. Reading to and with children helps them develop and enhance vocabulary which leads to improved comprehension. Table 3.9 summarizes strategies that can be used to teach reading at home.

Table 3.9 Summary of Strategies for Teaching Vocabulary in the Classroom and at Home

Conversation Strategies	
Family Activities	During family activities or experiences, provide simple explanations of the events and associated vocabulary in which your child may not be familiar. Example – While watching or playing soccer, explain that the referee makes sure that the rules of the game they are officiating are being followed by all players. Corner is a free kick from any of the four corners of the field. To shoot is to try and score a goal by kicking. These are just a few examples of vocabulary words that will provide background information and assist your child in gaining more meaning, but it will also assist in the learning of multiple-meaning words which will significantly enhance word knowledge.
Intentional Exposure to Different Words	After going on a walk, say something like: *"I'm parched"* as opposed to saying *"I'm thirsty"*. Your child will begin to use context clues to associate thirst with the word parched.
Stretch Your Vocabulary Game (during conversations)	Encourage your child to exchange a word for a synonym. Example – John was so mad when Lisa ate his candy. John was so __ ? John was so angry or John was furious.
Tall Tales	Creating a Tall-Tale is a creative way for children to use their imaginations with their new vocabulary word in a far out and totally unrealistically funny tale.

	Your child will really enjoy this activity and have a tale to associate with the word. If the parent participates as well and tries to outdo the child's tale or add to the child's tale, it will be even more fun and memorable.

Example – The new vocabulary word is journey. Today we went on a *journey* to the ocean. It took us five hours, but when we got there it was magical. We met an octopus who told us about a restaurant under the ocean that had the best hamburgers. We walked in the water, and immediately a whale picked us up and took us to the restaurant. When the whale dropped us off, an octopus greeted us and escorted us to our seats. He suggested we also order the ice cream and then go next door to see the starfish family. The starfish family took us on a ride around the ocean to meet all of the other animals. After meeting all of the animals, the whale picked us up again, but instead of taking us back to land, we sat on his head and the water from his blowhole blew us all the way back to our car. We then went back home and ended our *journey*. |
| **Read-Aloud Strategies** | |
| Books w/Unusual Language | ☐ Select books to read with rich and unusual language and varied levels of text. This will expose your child to a variety of different words and as a result, grow their vocabulary faster.
☐ When your child encounters an unfamiliar word, provide them with a kid-friendly definition and keep reading.

Here are two sources for kid friendly definitions:
☐ Miriam Webster's online Dictionary for Kids (http://learnersdictionary.com/)
☐ Collins Dictionary (collinsdictionary.com) |
| Mind Movies | ☐ Encourage your child to visualize what is happening in the story as you all are reading. The images or story line they are imagining is a Mind Movie. |

	☐ When reading an unfamiliar word, discuss how there is a break in the mind movie. Discuss the image, the meaning of the unfamiliar word, and the new image being visualized in the mind.
Context Clues (for unfamiliar words)	**Have you child reread the text to see if they can figure out the meaning of an unfamiliar word by the other words around the word.** Many times, authors include the definition of a word in the same sentence or near the word.
Ask Questions	During and after reading, ask your child questions to determine their comprehension of the texts. Specifically ask questions regarding new or unfamiliar words and concepts.
Kinesthetic-Tactile Strategies	
Act it Out	**When sharing a new word, have your child create an action or movement that is associated with the meaning.** The movement will assist your child with remembering the meaning of the word. Allow your child to come up with the movement, in order to have ownership of the word and meaning. **Example** – The new word is *accelerate*. The action or movement could be your child walking and then running across the room.
Synonym Match	**Use index cards to create a set of cards to play the traditional matching game.** ☐ On one card write a word and on the other a synonym. ☐ Create the number of card pairs based on the age or ability of your child. For young children, no more than five pair (10 cards). For older or more advanced children, 10 to 15 pair will be sufficient. **To play the game:** ☐ Mix the cards up and turn them face down.

	☐ Take turns trying to find the matching synonyms. If you find a match, your turn continues. The winner is the person with the most matches. *This game can be played using antonyms, homonyms or even definitions of words.* **Example** – Synonyms for Synonym Match – mad/angry; nice/kind; amazing/incredible; answer/respond
Vocabulary Rap	**Have your child to create a rap using their vocabulary terms.** This strategy works particularly well with upper elementary through high school children learning difficult concepts in social studies and science. Younger children can sing the definitions of terms to tunes such as *Happy Birthday* or *Twinkle, Twinkle Little Star.*)
Draw it Out	**Have your child to keep a word journal. In the journal, have your child:** ☐ Write the word ☐ Write a kid-friendly definition ☐ Write an example of the word ☐ Draw an image associated with the word. The image will help your child to remember the meaning of the word.

Conclusion

Vocabulary is a critical component in the process of learning to read. While there are a number of incidental strategies to teach vocabulary, the most beneficial is intentionally planned explicit instruction. Because the best and most aggressive reading programs teach an average of 10 – 12 words per week, it is important that vocabulary development becomes a part of all content areas and is integrated in all aspects of daily instruction. This can be done by using carefully structured routines and procedures and by utilizing word-learning strategies that build upon children's prior knowledge and personal experiences to make connections. This chapter provided many ideas that can be easily adapted and implemented, but the key is for teachers and parents to be creative, plan well, and make learning vocabulary fun and engaging.

CHAPTER FOUR

FLUENCY

Reading fluency refers to the ability of readers to read quickly, effortlessly, and efficiently with meaningful expression (Rasinski, 2006). It is evaluated at two levels: oral reading fluency and silent reading fluency. Fluent reading is not achieved in instructional experiences where the text is too difficult and when the reader struggles over words or develops decoding issues. Fluency is achieved through continued exposure to words by practicing reading a particular book. During a child's developmental stages, it is crucial for an educator or parent to monitor the child's progress to ensure he or she becomes fluent (Lapp & Moss, 2012). Those developmental stages include the foundational reading skills discussed in previous chapters, where we have referred to beginning readers as either children or learners. After children gain phonemic awareness, develop some phonics skills, and build their vocabularies, they can actually begin reading, therefore, moving forward, we will also refer to them as readers. This chapter focuses on strategies teachers and parents can use to help children/learners become fluent readers.

Understanding Fluency

Reading fluency has three main components: speed, accuracy, and prosody. Figure 4.1 explains each of these components. It is important for parents and educators to actively guide children through the process of reading with the correct pacing, accuracy, and expression, which will allow them to focus on comprehending what he or she is reading. Expression can be defined as the ability to change your voice to show emotion when reading.

Figure 4.1 Three Components of Reading Fluency

Speed -Fluent readers read at an appropriate rate for their age or grade level (usually measured in words per minute or wpm).
Accuracy- Fluent readers read words and phrases within a text with minimal mistakes.
Prosody- Fluent readers engage in expressive reading which focuses on timing, phrasing, emphasis, and intonation.

Fluency is a critical element of reading, since it forms a bridge between word recognition and comprehension. It gives readers time to concentrate on the meaning of the text. When a student can decode a specific text quickly and efficiently, they can recognize words with automaticity (Stanovich, 2000). Automaticity is the fast, effortless word recognition that is acquired through reading practice. Therefore, automaticity ensures the brain focuses more on the content of the text. This makes fluency one of the building blocks of reading, because it is directly linked to comprehension.

As noted in Figure 4.1, speed refers to reading at the appropriate rate for a reader's age or grade level. Accuracy accounts for the percentage of words read within a given text with minimal mistakes. In addition, teachers must measure prosody which includes the proper use of timing, phrasing, emphasis, and intonation. Refer to Figure 4.2 for explanations of the variables of prosody.

Fluency leads to more success with writing, proper vocabulary development, and greater comprehension. Researchers have recognized fluency as an essential component of proficient reading for some time, but some experts are concerned that fluency is still misunderstood or neglected.

Figure 4.2 Variables of Prosody

Intonation -the rise and fall of the voice when speaking/reading.
Rhythm-is the sense of movement in speech, marked by the stress, timing, and quantity of syllables.
Tone-a vocal sound with reference to its pitch, quality, and strength.
Stress -the force or emphasis used on a sound, syllable, or word in comparison to other sounds, syllables, or words in a sentence.

The automaticity theory was put forth by Dr. S. Jay Samuels (LaBerge & Samuels, 1974). It attempts to explain the relationship between fluency and comprehension. According to this theory, students have a limited amount of mental energy. A reader who must focus his or her attention on decoding words may not have enough mental energy left over to think about the meaning of the text. When readers employ their phonics skills, they are able to recognize familiar words quickly and figure out words they haven't previously encountered in a text.

The implication is that for a student to be a proficient reader, reading needs to become automatic in order for them to focus and pay attention to the text's meaning. When students are able to decode a given text at a fluent level, they are likely to apply metacognitive strategies that enable them to comprehend what they are reading (LaBerge & Samuels, 1974). For example, thinking aloud while reading is a metacognitive strategy that fluent readers use while engaging in the reading process.

One thing I've noticed as I've listened to students during guided reading and small group instruction is that students make the assumption that fluent reading means to read as fast as you can. For this reason, it is imperative to explain to students that reading at a good pace allows them to better understand what they are reading. If they are reading too fast, they may not be able to understand the text. Reading rate and comprehension of more complex text becomes less challenging as a student's knowledge of vocabulary increases. Nevertheless, every student does not find learning to read an easy task. Learning gaps may increase over time for students that face reading challenges. As a result, they may develop low morale and a lack of confidence.

Approach to Teaching Fluency in the Classroom

Teachers are integral to the journey towards developing readers' fluency skills. Teachers have to ensure that reading and comprehension activities that students participate in are valuable ones. To give students that much-needed support, and therefore improve their fluency skills, teachers can implement the strategies that will be discussed in this chapter. All strategies are summarized in Table 4.1 at the end of the chapter.

Teacher Modeling

From my experience in the classroom and observing other master teachers, teacher modeling is one strategy that is proven to be highly effective when providing fluency instruction. Teacher modeling, as it relates to fluency instruction, refers to instructional time when readers have the opportunity to listen to the teacher model what a fluent reader does when engaging with a text. In my own classroom, I often use the beginning of a guided reading lesson to model what fluent reading looks and sounds like. By listening to fluid examples, children are able to recognize how changes in voice can help them make sense of the text. An example of this would be using different voices when two or more characters are engaged in dialogue.

First, the teacher explains what fluent readers do while reading. Second, the teacher reads the text effortlessly and with expression. Third, after the read-aloud, the teacher asks readers what they noticed and encourages the readers to share their thoughts. Also, older readers may discuss how a fluent reader keeps the listener engaged. Teachers should remember to continually expose readers to various genres including poetry.

Echo Reading

Echo reading is an instructional strategy in which learners read a text after the teacher reads the text to enable learners to develop fluency and expression, as well as decoding abilities (Knoll, 2015). During this process, the teacher can model fluency and expressive reading by reading small chunks of text out loud. An example of this would be reading a paragraph to learners. The teachers and learners use copies of similar texts or a shared big book. After listening to the teacher, the learners read aloud from the same writing. This strategy bolsters the ability of turning printed text into spoken words and builds expression when reading aloud. Echo reading is most effective when dealing with short segments of a text and is better-suited for beginners

(Kuhn & Levy, 2015). The echo reading strategy is also helpful for struggling learners since it improves listening skills, builds confidence, vocabulary, comprehension, proper phrasing, and the identification of unknown words.

In echo reading, the teacher assists the learners in matching the spoken word with the printed word. To implement this type of instructional strategy in the classroom, the teacher should follow these steps:

1. First, select a predictable text with limited print, then read the text to the students.
2. Second, the teacher should ensure the learner tracks the text with his or her eyes (Griffith, 2008).
3. Third, the learner should recite the text or passage back to the teacher.
4. Next, the teacher reads the next paragraph or sentence, and the learner repeats the sentence. The procedure is repeated until fluency is achieved.

During the process, if the reader makes an error or hesitates while reading, the teacher should note those mistakes and mark them as an area for improvement. When mistakes are noticed, the teacher should politely say "stop", point to the error word, and say the word correctly. The learner should then repeat the word, then backtrack and reread the whole sentence (Kuhn & Levy, 2015). Echo reading should be repeated until readers master the problematic word(s).

Choral Reading

Choral reading is a technique where all the learners in a class Read-Aloud and in unison from the same text. It happens with or without the help of the teacher (Paige, 2011). In cases where the teacher participates in choral reading, the teacher models the accurate pronunciation of words and the correct rate of reading and expression. It helps the learners build their reading fluency, self-confidence, and motivation. Finally, choral reading also allows the teacher to model decoding by reviewing problematic words and phrases (Mink & Deborah, 2009). This technique is essential, as it enables readers to improve their decoding ability and thus leads to more fluent reading.

The choral reading instructional strategy is very flexible and allows teachers to choose a variety of texts at all grade levels. First, the teacher should choose a book or a passage that is at or between all readers' independent reading levels and instructional reading levels, so that the text is challenging but still manageable for all. The text should be long enough to offer a two-minute reading at an appropriate reading rate; however, the text should not be too long. The optimal length is between 200 and 250 words.

Second, if it is at all possible, the teacher should provide all readers a copy of the same text so they can follow along. The text can come in the form of a book, handout, or can be projected on the board. Third, the teacher should read the text aloud and model fluent reading for the learners (Wagstaff, 1994). The teacher should move about the classroom and encourage all readers to participate. If the passage is provided on a handout, the teacher can ask the readers to use a highlighter to follow along with the text as they read.Finally, the teacher should direct readers in reading the text aloud and in unison. After the reading, the teacher should give corrective feedback but should not single out any specific reader for appropriate or inappropriate reading (Mink & Deborah, 2009). The input should be directed at the whole class.

Repeated Reading

Repeated reading is a fluency technique where readers read a selected passage over and over again, aloud or silently (Rasinski, Blachowicz & Lems, 2012). Teachers generally use this strategy to improve readers' fluency (Rasinski, 2005). Repeated reading is continued until the reader can complete the passage fluently without making errors. The essence of repeated reading is to promote fluency as well as comprehension. This technique can be implemented in a group or with one reader. Repeated reading is essential to readers whose skills are accurate yet choppy, by assisting them in developing automaticity, or by ensuring they read quickly and accurately.

In implementing this academic intervention, the only tools required are the selected text and maybe a timer. The teacher can employ repeated reading by implementing a few simple steps. First, take the learners to a quiet area where there will be little or no distractions. Make sure the book can be easily viewed by both the learner and the teacher (Bender & Larkin, 2003). It may be more comfortable for the learners and the teacher to each have their own copy of the passage. The chosen passage should be about 150-250 words in length, depending on the learners' reading levels. Next, the teacher should listen to the learners read the text. After each reading, the teacher offers feedback related to accuracy, phrasing, rate, and/or expression. The reader should read the text three times, each time the student monitors where they stopped. The goal, at the end of each reading, should be for readers to recognize an increase in accuracy of words read at an appropriate rate with expression. Lastly, readers should graph their growth on a student fluency tracker. A variety of fluency trackers can be found online by conducting a simple Google® search.

Approach to Teaching Fluency at Home

Read-Alouds

Early exposure is the most crucial aspect of language development and learning to read. There are numerous reasons why you should read to your child daily. By reading together every day, you can stimulate and develop a child's language and literacy skills (Williams & Giordano, 2019). Children can love the sound of a language before noticing the existence of printed words. Reading aloud to children arouses their ability to imagine, thus, expanding their understanding of their environment. It prepares children to comprehend written words (Williams & Giordano, 2019). As the rhythm and melody of a language become part of a child's life, learning to read becomes as natural as learning to walk and talk.

Reading aloud to children also builds healthy brain development and fosters early learning. Reading aloud makes connections in the brain, which promote language, cognitive, and social and emotional development (Mackenzie, 2018). By reading with your child, you help cultivate an everlasting love for reading, Reading to young children increases their attention spans, enabling them to perform well in many school subjects and everyday life.

Reading aloud and discussing texts with your child increases their problem-solving abilities and builds good comprehension. Children who have been read to are ordinarily adept at creating stories from their imaginations. The imagination is fueled by reading aloud, so the power of the child's imagination is also strengthened (Mackenzie, 2018). When children listen to an adult reading to them, they can develop strong language skills that assist in language development. Reading aloud to children also supports them in becoming more

fluent readers. Finally, reading to your child provides an opportunity fosr the parent and child to bond. The more children read or are read to, the more they are likely to develop as readers. It is recommended that beginners spend 15 to 20 minutes reading daily (Baker, Dreher & Guthrie, 2000). It is crucial to note, however, that if a child is interested in and enjoys what she or he is reading, it is good to encourage even more reading time.

Table 4.1 Summary of Fluency Strategies to Implement in the Classroom

Classroom Fluency Strategy	How to Implement the Strategy
Model Fluent Reading	☐Teacher explains what fluent readers do while reading. ☐Teacher reads the text with expression. ☐After the read-aloud, the teacher asks readers what they noticed and encourages the readers to share their thoughts.
Echo Read	☐Select a predictable text with limited print. ☐Read the text to the students. Teacher ensures the learner tracks the text with his or her eyes. ☐Learner should read the text after the teacher. ☐Teacher reads the next paragraph or sentence, and then the learner reads it. ☐Repeat these steps until fluency is achieved.
Choral Read	☐Choose a passage that is at or near the readers' independent reading levels. ☐Provide all students a copy of the passage. ☐Read the passage or aloud and model fluent reading for the students. ☐Students should use a pointing finger to track the text as they read. ☐Students read the passage aloud simultaneously.
Repeated Reading	☐Choose a passage no more than 150- 250 words in length. ☐Teacher should listen to the student read the text. ☐After each reading offer the student feedback related to accuracy, phrasing, rate, and/or expression. ☐Student should read the text three times, each time the student records where they stopped.

Audio-Assisted Reading

Listening to and following along with an audio recording of a book is known as audio-assisted reading. It is a reading strategy where learners read together in their books while hearing or listening to a fluent reader read the book on an audio recording device such as an iPad, audio-book, or a reading app like Tumblebooks. Once the learners develop confidence and improve their reading skills, they can read the same text without the assistance of the audio recording device.

There are many benefits attached to audio-assisted reading. This strategy assists readers in building specific fluency skills like proper expressions, as well as phrasing of sentences. It also enables readers to improve on sight word recognition. Further, readers can hear the tone and pace of a more skilled reader (Lems, Miller & Soro, 2017).

Audio-assisted reading activities provide a significant boost to building reading comprehension. Above all, this is a flexible method that can be employed across all content areas. Audio-assisted reading should be used when working with children who are just starting to learn how to read. Parents should choose a book with an audio-recording of the text, which is slightly above the reader's independent reading level (Rasinski & Padak, 2013). The parent will then have the reader listen to an accompanying audio recording while following along with the written copy of the text. The reader should then read out aloud along with the audio recording. Parents should then allow the learner an opportunity to read the book without the audio (Rasinski & Padak, 2013). Finally, the reader should read the text again and again, along with the sound, until they become comfortable reading the text without audio assistance.

Sight Words

Sight words are commonly-used words that young children are encouraged to keep in their memory by sight. Once the child memorizes sight words, they can recognize them in print without using any instruction(al) strategy (Flora, 2007). The skill of remembering and recognizing sight words is called sight word recognition.

The basic premise is that sight words are words that are not decoded, but are read by sight. There are also irregular sight words, which are words that cannot be decoded and don't follow the traditional English spelling rules. In my experience working with young readers, an effective and engaging way to approach sight word instruction is learning through play. Table 4.2 includes several example of how children can learn sight words through play.

Conclusion

The aforementioned teaching strategies will allow readers to practice the skills needed to develop fluency. Teachers and parents are encouraged to seek out additional strategies to implement from the vast amount of available literacy resources. Teachers and parents can implement a combination of strategies so readers will have more opportunities to improve their skills. There are many different approaches that can be used. The strategy that will work best depends on the reader's preferences, as well as the amount of time that is spent providing the student with reading instruction and support. Refer to Table 4.4 for additional resources to support teaching reading fluency.

Table 4.2 Strategies for Learning Sight Words through Play

Sight Word Play Strategy	How to Implement Sight Word Play Strategy
See & Say	The reader views the sight word on the flash card and says the word.
Spell & Read	The reader says the word, spells it out then reads the word again.
Sand Writing	The reader says the word then spells it out in a tray of sand.
Magnetic Letters	The reader says the word and uses magnetics to spell it out.
Hide & Seek	☐Choose no more than 25 sight words. ☐Write each word on an index card. ☐Hide the cards in various places. ☐As the child finds and picks up each card, they must say the word. ☐If the child says the wrong word, gently correct them and continue the game.
Memory	☐Choose no more than 20 sight words. ☐Write each word on two index cards. ☐Lay the cards face down and have the child choose two cards at a time. ☐Each time the child picks up a card, they must read the words to see if the cards match. ☐If the child says the wrong word gently correct them and continue the game. ☐The reader with the most matches wins the game (if multiple children are playing at the same time).

Table 4.3 Fluency Strategies to Implement at Home

At-Home Fluency Strategy	How to Implement At-Home Fluency Strategy
Read-Aloud	☐Choose a book of your child's interest to read-aloud. ☐Discuss the text with your child. ☐Have your child read the text to you. ☐Monitor their accuracy, expression, and pace while reading. ☐Provide support as needed.
Audio-Assisted Reading	☐Choose a book and audio-recording of the text you select. ☐Have your child listen to an audio as they follow along with the written copy of the text. ☐The child should then read out aloud along with the audio recording. ☐Allow the child to read the book without the audio recording.
Sight-Word Practice	Try the Sight Word Play Strategies described in Table 4.2.

Table 4.4 Additional Resources to Support Reading Fluency Instruction

Title of Resource	URL	Description
Fountas and Pinnell's *Sing a Song of Poetry: A Teaching Resource for Phonemic Awareness, Phonics, and Fluency*	www.fountasandpinnell.com	This book provides a plethora of poems to read to and with students.
2017 Hasbrouck & Tindal Oral Reading Norms	https://www.readingrockets.org/sites/default/files/2017%20ORF%20NORMS.pdf	Use the information in this table to draw conclusions and make decisions about the oral reading fluency of your students.
Sight Words by TS Apps		Sight Word App
Choral Reading Video by Reading Rockets	https://youtu.be/o_-z8d0sRUA	Choral reading is reading aloud in unison with a whole class or group of students. Choral reading helps build students' fluency, self-confidence, and motivation.
Repeated Reading Video by www.HelpforReading.com.	https://youtu.be/NSD8KQDPjDU	Repeated reading is a technique to help a child's growth in reading fluency.
How to Teach Fluency with Accuracy and Phrasing Video by McGraw-Hill Prek-12	https://youtu.be/oEc9u4oO4nc	This video shows a teacher conducting a fluency activity in which students focus on accuracy and phrasing. This short video is great for teachers looking to teach fluency in their classroom
Building Reading Fluency for the Young Black Child by SCA Tutoring Center	https://www.teacherspayteachers.com/Product/BUILDING-READING-FLUENCY-FOR-THE-YOUNG-BLACK-CHILD-5651039?fbclid=IwAR3Y5jq4N8mif_W7yQcHcnKZ5Oal9WfOkBDbw2fuApl1j2on2IHIRXX0HjU	This workbook will help develop and build fluent, confident readers! Includes easy-to-read passages designed to uplift our children as well as develop the skills needed to become a fluent reader.
Little Blue Truck Read-aloud	https://youtu.be/vt1Twhs8KiA	Children are encouraged to echo read during this read-aloud.
Buzz Said the Bee Read-aloud	https://youtu.be/KCFFqKA85lE	Children are encouraged to read along with author
Easy CBM	https://dibels.uoregon.edu/assessment/reading	Easy CBM addressed. Skill sets include: Letter Names, Phoneme Segmenting, Letter Sounds, Word Reading Fluency, Passage Reading Fluency, and Multiple Choice Reading Comprehension
Think Fluency Assessment App	http://www.thinkfluency.com/	ThinkFluency is a reading fluency assessment tool for teachers who want to spend less time assessing and more time teaching.

CHAPTER FIVE

COMPREHENSION

How many of us just want to understand what is happening in the world? Why people have certain jobs? Or simply want to know, of everything that we see on the news or in the media, what it all *really* means? Comprehension is a foundational skill that can be described as an active process in which an individual understands spoken, written, and/or visual texts (Shanahan & Shanahan, 2012). True comprehension results when an individual can make sense of what is presented.

This foundational skill is necessary to empower students as they develop cognitively. It is imperative that students' reading be purposeful. Students must become active readers that can fully engage with the text. In order to accurately understand reading material, students must be able to decode what they read, make connections to prior knowledge, and think critically about content (Harvey & Goudvis, 2017). We have all heard the saying, 'reading is fundamental,' and it *really* is. Reading, with understanding, can serve as a catalyst to unlock students' potential. It's not so much about passing standardized assessments, but more so about how what one reads can impact how they view themselves and the world.

Teaching comprehension is no easy feat. As an educator, you must know your students' Lexile scores, and how to differentiate instruction for all learners, while addressing the required standards, as identified by your state's department of education. None of these speak to the deficits students may come to you with.

Though the current literacy rate in the United States is 99%, there are 45 million Americans that are functionally illiterate with the inability to read above a 5th grade level (The Literacy Project, 2017). Cognitive processes develop rapidly from birth to three, 85% of the brain is developed by the age of three (Schweinhart et al., 2005). Now what does this mean for the highly efficacious educator? We must bridge the opportunity, achievement, and cultural gaps in order to cultivate lifelong learners.Research-based instructional strategies are essential to a student, teacher, and school's success. In order to attain the goal, teachers must be aware of where their students are, in relation to where they should be, and the best instructional practices to use to help get them there. There is *"no one size fits all"* approach to meeting the needs of scholars, but there are some best practices that will lighten the load of increasing students' ability to comprehend text. Use of formative assessments help teachers identify what students know, can do, and understand. Skillful teachers will use data from these assessments to inform instruction, build cooperative groups, and personalize instruction. Comprehension is a universal tool to understanding everything. Whether it is introducing a new topic, building prior knowledge or analyzing a photo, understanding "what is," is core.

ROWLS is an acronym I use for the dimensions of literacy: **R**eading, **O**bserving, **W**riting, **L**istening, and **S**peaking. For example, one universal theme in social studies is conflict and change. In order to teach concepts around COVID-19, a teacher could assign students, at any grade level to watch the news and observe what they see, reflect on what they heard, and write out how it made them feel.

Though there are many conflicts, a younger student can share that they cannot go to school or a playground, a middle age student may share that many people are dying, where as an older student may share, the government has not identified a cure or have a solid response to the country's economy. The discussion the following day could be the teacher probing students on what has changed since, the onset of COVID-19 (i.e. no school, business hours changing, required to wear masks, etc.). The teacher must take an active role in teaching students, at all ages, *how* to think, not *what* to think.

Approach to Teaching Comprehension in the Classroom

The eight dimensions of comprehension include: connecting, inferring, visualizing, questioning, determining importance, synthesizing, predicting, and summarizing. This chapter will explore eight skills that can assist students' ability to effectively comprehend text.

Connecting

Teachers must create opportunities for students to relate to what they are learning. There are three ways for students to connect: text-to-self, text-to-text, and text-to-world (Shea & Ceprano, 2017). These three connections assist students with not only understanding what is being read, but also helps them to chunk information. Examples of each form of connecting can be found in Table 5.1.

To help students to connect to the text, students should learn how to incorporate prior knowledge into their reading. Background knowledge is a powerful tool to help learners connect to the text. Through background knowledge, students can connect text to memories and experiences using visualization. For example, with text-to-self connections I provide students with a blank sheet of paper and have them write the five senses (hearing, seeing, smelling, feeling, and tasting). Next, I have students write words, phrases, or draw pictures to connect their prior knowledge to the current text topic with their five senses.

When connecting text-to-text learners should be given time to think about the text and key details or information from the text. Students should write out some things that come to their mind as they are reflecting on the first text. Student will do the same for the second text. Students are then ready to reflect on the connections between the two texts. Teachers should enhance the understanding of text-to-text connections by posing questions. Chunking the completion time provides learners with more thinking time, reduces non-preferred behaviors, and helps students to maintain focus for completion and understanding.

Making text-to-world connections is usually the most difficult connection type for learners. This is difficult for students because they may not have yet learned how to build upon their background knowledge. Now is the perfect time to teach students text-to-world connections considering the numerous protests taking place all of the United States this year. See Table 5.1 for a practical example of how this can be done. Building prior knowledge is important for students to understand how to make connections to the text they read. The ability to build on prior knowledge is also important when inferring.

Table 5.1 Examples of Three Connection Types

Type of Connection	Example
Text to Self	☐ Model this connection type using the original *Three Little Pigs* and Kyle Exum's version, which is a more modern, culturally-relevant version. Students can make connections by relating this to things they have experience with like Fortnite, McDonald's, having asthma, etc. ☐ Have the students identify the similarities and differences between the texts, through use of a *Double Bubble Thinking Map.* Students are likely to be heavily engaged due to the cultural relevance. Equally important is the students' ability to share experiences to self, others and the world.
Text to Text	☐ Provide learners with a Venn diagram to help with organizing their ideas. ☐ Give learners time to think about any key details or information from the first text and write them out. ☐ Next, learners will think about any key details or information from the second text and write them out. ☐ Allow students to reflect on the two texts. Completing the Venn Diagram should be chunked over time.
Text to World	☐ Use the book *I am Martin Luther King, Jr* by Brad Meltzer (2016), or something similar, with your students. ☐ Talk with students about the protests taking place in 2020 and the events leading up to them. ☐ Allow students to make the connection of standing up against racism through protesting from the text to what they seeing on television or witnessing in their own community.

Inferring

"Listening with your eyes and ears" comes to mind when thinking about inferring as a skill. Students must be taught to read between the lines. This skill can be defined as a comprehension strategy that helps students understand what is not explicitly stated (Ozgungor & Guthrie, 2004). Marzano (2010) described inference as a prerequisite to higher-order thinking in the 21st century. Observations are critical to making inferences and drawing conclusions. Furthermore, Marzano (2010) provided the following four questions to engage students in a discussion regarding inferences:

1. What is my inference?
2. What information did I use to make this inference?
3. How good was my thinking? And
4. Do I need to change my thinking?

As a classroom teacher, I always greeted students at the door with a smile and personalized greeting. My students knew this. If ever there was not a "welcome," there were issues. To introduce inferences, when the last three students entered the classroom, I was overly excited for student A, completely ignored student B, and was overly mean to student C (prior permission was given). The Do Now, for the day, was to describe what was observed and formulate perspectives based on knowledge. This ignited the conversation on how to make conclusions on what one has observed, knows, and the information provided. Students must be taught how to use context clues, from the text, observations, prior knowledge, and schema. Giving students different scenarios to analyze and share can help students build their inference skills. Character traits, one's ability to identify cause and effect, and the use of context clues to fully understand text. Pictures and visual aids also great ways to teach inference. One strategy could be to have students to look at one image and come up with three different descriptive explanations based on what is seen.

Learners require repetition of the inference skills previously mentioned, which can often require ongoing teacher support to help them to identify context clues. You can make sure students understand the literal facts from the story by reviewing and questioning student background knowledge. When students struggle with reading between the lines, they often struggle with discriminating ideas and responding to questions. A great strategy to used to build the background knowledge of learners is using anticipation guides. Anticipation guides are pre/post documentation guides to help students build on prior knowledge of a new topic. Jacobs (2010) describes anticipation guides as discovery of one's own thoughts and opinions. Anticipation guides can be designed for students of all ages and abilities and can include the use of images, audio, and other accommodations. When teaching inference, I have found that anticipation guides provide students with a visual organizer to express their thinking.

Visualizing

Albert Einstein once said, 'If I can't picture it, I can't understand it.' Students enjoy reading when they can fully grasp what's happening. Visualizing occurs when a person takes what they read and create pictures in their head (Wilson, 2014). Visualization requires students to utilize background knowledge, their imagination, and the context of the text to formulate images. Students' ability to do this helps them with recall, connections, inquiry, and deep comprehension. For students that struggle with understanding, visualizing helps students get a feel of how characters look and act.

One easy way to assist students with this skill is use of their five senses. Based on what students have read, ask them "what do you see, hear, feel, smell, and/or taste?" Addressing the diverse modalities of students' learning is an easy feat with visualizations. You can play a soundscape and have students create a mental image reflective of each of the five senses. This can easily be addressed with use of the 3-2-1 instructional strategy. Based on what they've read and using 3 of the 5 senses, have students provide 3 descriptive words for what they see, 2 words about what they feel, and 1 word for what they would hear if they were there. Have students to identify their favorite place in the world, and describe what they might see, hear, smell, feel, and taste.

Along with using the five senses, learners require repetitive, multi-sensory experiences to aid in visualizing text. Providing multi-sensory experiences before, during, and after reading gives learners more exposure with the visualization of text. In my experience providing reading instruction to learners at all levels, I have found that it is often difficult for some students to use visualization strategies when attempting to comprehend reading text. According to Park (2012), understanding new perspectives in reading is often difficult for learners because they are unable to cross-examine their thoughts.

To teach visualization to learners, I have experienced great success with reading descriptive sentences and having students close their eyes and visualize what is happening. For example, I might inform students that I am going to read a sentence about a student experience with COVID-19. After providing this information, I ask the students to clear their minds and close their eyes. I want my student to feel like they are a part of the story. I then read "It is now eleven o'clock in the morning, I am on the fourth floor of this lonely hospital and I have not seen or heard anyone all day. Suddenly, a tall man wearing a mask walks into the room wearing a long white coat and glasses. He is fair skinned, with brown eyes, brown hair, and a pointy nose. He walks over to a whiteboard on the wall and writes COVID-19". These descriptive sentences paint an image in the student's minds on what is happening in the story. Some students may believe they know the race of the character that walked into the room and a conversation on race may spark. According to Park (2012), "inviting students to visualize literacy characters is another way to initiate conversation on race". Another important consideration is the setting. All students may not have ever been in a hospital room so the conversation on visualization may lead to the next strategy, which is questioning.

Questioning

Questioning is one of the most critical components of comprehension. This skill requires students to engage or interact with the text. Questioning should occur before, during, and after reading the text. Asking questions before reading allows students to activate prior knowledge, while predicting what will happen.

Figure 5.1 Before Reading Questions

Is the story fiction or nonfiction? Did you look at the clues in the title and pictures? What do you already know about this topic? Can you predict meaning of new vocabulary? What questions do you have based on the topic? Do you know who the main character is and what needs they may have? What do you predict the story is about? What do you think you will learn?

Teachers can also use questioning during reading to build academic and technical vocabulary. Vocabulary development requires students to understand prefixes and suffixes, as well as understand the multiple meanings of words based on the context. Alexander (2020) shared vocabulary is significant to students' reading success for three primary reasons: knowing what words means improves comprehension, "words are the currency of communication" (p. 1), and academic and social competence and confidence is enhanced when students' vocabulary improves. Reading a text not only builds vocabulary, but also meaning of the text.

Figure 5.2 During Reading Questions

What do you predict will happen next? How do you predict the story will end? What questions do you have about the characters? Which parts of this story don't you understand? Did you re-read the text to understand confusing parts? Does the story remind you of anything in your life? What parts do you think are important?

After reading questions are just as important as questions asked before and during the text. This is how you, as a teacher, can determine if the students comprehend what they have read. The easiest way to begin this phase is to answer: who, what, where, when, why and how. Teachers can then ask questions that make connections between occurrences in the text. Further, teachers can ask higher-order thinking questions using the stem, "if...then..." This requires the students to think outside of the box. For example, If the Articles of Confederation, were not replaced by the Constitution, then what would happen regarding the government's financing during the COVID19 pandemic? Ideally, students would say Congress would have no power to levy or collect taxes, so there would be no stimulus checks. One last component regarding after reading questions, would be to ask questions based on different perspective and see how responses may vary. Students must know that perspective matters.

Figure 5.3 After Reading Checklist

What do you think is the main idea of the text?
What do you think the author is trying to tell you?
How did the story or text make you feel?
Were the predictions you made right or wrong?
How would you rewrite or retell the sequence of events?
What clues in the text help you to understanding the meaning of the story?
What evidence from the text can you identify to prove your points?

Questioning allows learners to connect with the text. Learners often require step by step modeling of questioning strategies. Providing students with accessible question stems and anchor charts is a great way to do this. To teach questioning to learners before reading, first model the expectation. For example, after introducing the book *The Invisible Boy* by Patrice Barton, model questioning by answering questions and allowing students to share their opinions. You might ask students what they think the book is about by looking at the cover illustration and title. Then, answer the question by telling the students *"I think this book is about a boy who thinks he is invisible"*. You might also ask learners what they think they will learn from the book prior to reading it. Then, model answering that question by letting telling the students, *"I think I will learn how I can be aware of others and accept them for who they are"*.

During reading, continue to model the expectation of using questions for reading comprehension. Begin with asking questions about the main character in the text. In the story *The Invisible Boy*, the main character is Brian. Use questioning to start a conversation about

Brian by asking students the following questions and answering them yourself:

1. Do you think Brian is an invisible boy?
2. Why would Brian feel invisible if he is in the same class as other students?
3. What questions do you have about Brian?
4. So far, does this story remind you of your life?

Continue to ask questions throughout the story to help students understand the story and continue to use visualization to support this strategy. Also emphasize that questioning is important because it checks our comprehension of the text.

After reading the story, check in with the students to assess their thoughts, opinions, and understanding of the text. Use and model questioning to ask follow-up questions and to provide students with opportunities for higher-order thinking. For the picture book, *The Invisible Boy*, ask students why did Brian felt like he was invisible and why the story ended the way it did? Questioning learners will also help students with the next reading comprehension strategy, which is determining importance.

Determining Importance

Have you ever been reading a text and after you finished, asked yourself, *"was all of that necessary?"* or thought *"the author could have just said..."* Determining importance is simply described as focusing on what is most important within a text. What we, as educators have to be mindful of is young students must be taught this skill, because in the lower grades, they typically believe everything is important.

As a middle school teacher, I remember getting new text books my first year and getting in trouble when I turned them back in, because I taught my students to highlight everything in the book that may not be true or that could not be proven. That year, my students and I were unable to find any textual evidence to support "weapons of mass destruction", thus, almost half of their textbooks were a rainbow of colors (from highlights and annotations). My students were taught that if you cannot prove something, it may not be true, therefore, conducting research is essential. Almost every assignment in that class was a research project, based on the curriculum.

Teaching importance involves teaching children how to identify big ideas and organize their thinking, while nurturing their creativity. Teaching how to determine importance is an interdisciplinary strategy; however, with younger kids, it is sometimes easier to start within the context of science and social studies (Gunning, 2012). Research- or inquiry-based learning sparks the act of questioning which lends itself to wanting to know more about a concept. Determining importance starts with differentiation between details and big ideas. Students must learn how details support the big idea and add value to understanding the text. Active and continuous note-taking should occur while determining importance. Distinguishing between fact and opinion is also critical to the developing of this skill.

Determining significance, or importance, in fictional and non-fictional texts requires a different approach. Graphic organizers, such as thinking maps, can be used for both. Understanding the structure of a fictional text is the key to determining significance. The five primary dimensions of fictional texts, as defined by Harvey & Goudvis (2017) are listed in Figure 5.4.

Figure 5.4 Five Primary Dimensions of Fictional Texts

Background knowledge: Learning about the characters and the setting of the story. **Rising action:** Identifying the main events leading up to the problem (climax). **Climax:** The main problem in the story; biggest action; the point at which the story changes. **Falling action:** Reactions to the problem or solutions to occur. **Solution and conclusion:** When the problem is solved.

Unlike fictional texts, that for the most part have a simple structure, non-fictional text structure varies greatly. These texts structures can be sequential (specific order or step-by-step), descriptive (detail -oriented), problem and solution (problem, supporting events, solution), compare and contrast (how things are similar and different), and cause and effect (how something happening impacts something else). Readers have to be able to identify what the author wants them to learn, what information is essential, and what is interesting (but not essential).

Readers must be explicitly taught to determine importance. For many learners, it is difficult to distinguish important information from information that does not aid in comprehension. Only some of the information in the text is important for comprehension. The rest of it is there to provide details and make the text more interesting. Essentially, determining importance is the same as looking for the big idea.

The first step in teaching determining importance is to provide students with visual aids. This can be done several different ways. One way to use a visual aid to teach determining importance is by providing students with a group of visual cards. The cards should have pictures on a related or unrelated topic. Students are asked to determine which of the pictures are important and which pictures are just details. For example, when learning about making a bowl of cereal, have pictures of a cereal box, a toothbrush, a washcloth, a bowl, a spoon, and milk. The students have to determine which items are important for making a bowl of cereal. Students should able to easily rule out a toothbrush and a washcloth because these items do not directly relate to making a bowl of cereal. Another visual representation activity is described in Figure 5.5.

Figure 5.5 Determining Importance Visual Representation Graphic Organizer Activity

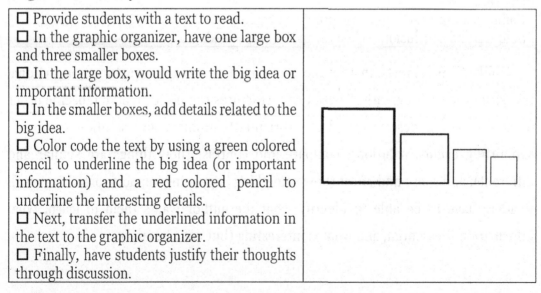

☐ Provide students with a text to read.
☐ In the graphic organizer, have one large box and three smaller boxes.
☐ In the large box, would write the big idea or important information.
☐ In the smaller boxes, add details related to the big idea.
☐ Color code the text by using a green colored pencil to underline the big idea (or important information) and a red colored pencil to underline the interesting details.
☐ Next, transfer the underlined information in the text to the graphic organizer.
☐ Finally, have students justify their thoughts through discussion.

Learners should be exposed to multiple strategies for determining importance in both fiction and non-fiction text. When using fiction text students should be taught to locate important information in the story using the five dimensions of fictional text. Students should also be guided to look for details about the characters, setting, and events. When looking at the character or characters, students should be aware of the character's languages, actions, and relationships, as well as, the affect the character has on the story plot. Students should be directed on how the setting contributes to what is happening in the story. When looking at events, teach students how the event influences the story by directing students to locate problems and solutions within the text. With nonfiction text, students must use text features, vocabulary, details, topic sentences, and an understanding of text structure to determine importance within text. This information coupled with background knowledge will also help students with synthesizing.

Synthesizing

Synthesizing can be described as, "the process through which readers bring together their background knowledge and their evolving understanding of the text" (Miller, 2013, p.171). Synthesizing can occur without it being explicitly taught by using the two methods below:

- Ask Questions: Have students answer questions about a text.
- Build/Activate Schema: Students create a diagram or develop an analogy that represents the concept

Each requires students to take what they know and have read, and use it to advance their thinking to produce a response or illustration of their new understanding. Students must combine what they already know with what they are reading to formulate new ideas.

Like determining importance, synthesizing varies with fiction and nonfiction texts. Synthesizing students' thinking can occur through the use of the following phrases:

- in the beginning I thought
- then I thought
- now, I am thinking

One helpful trick would be to help students create images for each thought process. In informational texts, synthesis occurs typically at the culmination of the inquiry. This is the result of the use of a multiplicity of texts (i.e. different books, videos, news clips, primary and secondary texts on the same topic). Synthesizing allows for a reader's continual understanding of text.

Teaching synthesizing to learners requires multi-step instruction. Students should use questioning of thoughts, characters, events, and the story setting when reading the beginning, middle and end of the text. Learners must be taught how to think strategically. Before reading the story, students should be asked to reflect on their prior knowledge of the topic. Learners should share those thoughts verbally and in writing. Next, students should read or listen to the first part of the text and reflect on new thoughts or misconceptions of the topic. This should be repeated as they read more of the book. At the end of the book, students should discuss their thoughts and misconceptions in further details. Students can apply these steps when using other forms of text or media on a topic.

Predicting

Students' ability to use information (i.e. titles, headings, pictures and diagrams) from the text to anticipate what will happen in the text is described as predictions (Bailey, 2015). Students must actively engage in the text, to use prior knowledge to think ahead and ask questions they expect to be answered throughout their reading as well as how they presume the story will end. Use of this strategy requires students to consistently reflect on what they have read and what they know. Teachers can start with having students to complete a scavenger hunt about a text they are going to read and have students think, pair, and share regarding the content of the text.

Predictions are used by great readers to connect knowledge with information from the text. For this, students must be engaged from text selection to after the reading. At the beginning, students should explain what they think and justify it. The reading process for prediction includes the following:

- Before: Examine title and illustrations
- During: Take random pauses and predict what will have next
- After: Confirm or adjust predictions, based on new knowledge

What helps with students fine-tuning their craft is use of text with cultural relevance and/or students' interests.

Predictions require students to use prior knowledge. "Using strategies to activate prior knowledge will support effective prediction and comprehension" (Duke & Pearson, 2001). Predicting what a text is about by looking at the title and cover illustrations is a great way to activate prior knowledge for learners. Once prior knowledge is activated, the book should be read with frequent pauses. The pauses should be used to reflect on what was read and predict what is going to happen next. Students should also utilize pauses from text to hone in on previous predictions and, if necessary, modify those predictions. An example of how this strategy has been used is detailed in Figure 5.6.

Figure 5.6 Description of Lesson Using Predicting Strategy

Using the text, *The Sandwich Swap* by Queen Rania Al Abdullah & Kelly DiPucchio (2010)
☐ Present the title and the cover page to students and ask them to make a prediction on what the story is going to be about.
☐ During the conflict in the story, when the two characters thought each other sandwiches looked disgusting, ask the students to make another prediction on what is going to happen next. (Students should use their previous predictions along with new predictions to try to determine how the story will end.)
☐ At the end of the story, the students will able to confirm whether or not their predictions were accurate.

During this lesson, prior to the start of reading, many students predicted that the girls would swap sandwiches. Although that did happen, the students had to read the story to see that this swap would affect the whole school. After reading the text, students were able to provide a summary of their predictions and what happened in the story.

Summarizing

The final primary comprehension strategy is summarizing. Summarizing helps students discern big ideas from irrelevant ones, while integrating central ideas in a meaningful way (Stahl, 2004). The goal of every teacher is to ensure students can recall what they have read and make sense of the information. Summarization includes one's ability to identify key elements of the story, condense significant details into one's own words and solidify understanding and meaning. This skill cannot be done with fidelity without students being able to determine significance. It is easy for students to pull out details and miss the main idea. This strategy must be explicitly taught and modeled to ensure students' success.

Like some of the other strategies, there is a varied approach when summarizing a fictional text, compared to a nonfiction text. In fiction, the focus of the texts are the basic story elements (previously described in the chapter) , whereas in a nonfiction text, the focus is to coherently gather the most important information about a topic. One easy way to summarize a text is to complete the "who, what, when, where, how and why" of the text. This can be done by chapter or section. To add value, you can have students create images to support the information they chose to highlight. This can be tied into some of the other skills (i.e. connecting, visualizing, inferring, determining importance, and synthesizing). Another strategy to address this skill is use of the Jigsaw strategy. The teacher assigns pairs or groups of students to complete a reading assignment and then has them share the information out. To ensure that students can make connections between each section, teachers can require students to create a "big picture" summarizing all sections into one.

When teaching summarizing to learners it is crucial that teachers select the correct text, model, and provide graphic organizers. Text should be easy to comprehend. Students cannot summarize what they cannot comprehend. Teachers should model the expectations of summarizing the text. Students should also be informed that their summary should include information from the text rather than their own thoughts and ideas about the text. Using graphic organizers can help students to organize their thoughts. When summarizing text graphic organizers should be utilized in a procedural way. Students should know when and how to fill in each portion of the graphic organizer. "Students often have difficulty deciding what is important in the text and putting it in their own words. Summarizing can be highly effective in helping students identify main ideas, generalize, remove redundancy, integrate ideas, and improve their memory of what they have read" (Zygouris-Coe, 2009). When summarizing is taught appropriately, all learners will learn to successfully summarize text.

In this section of this chapter, we have addressed the importance of comprehension, strategies to assist with comprehension, and examples of how to implement each strategy for all learners. We hope educators use this information to help students become more successful at comprehending all text. Comprehension helps us to understand the world around us. Comprehension is a foundational reading skill that can boost a student's cognitive abilities in all content areas.

It is imperative to future learning that students have a solid understanding of comprehension. As educators, we must do our part to ensure that students comprehend text by developing previously taught foundational skills such as decoding, vocabulary, and fluency. "One of the best predictors of a child's ability to comprehend print is his or her ability to decode print" (Trehearne & Healy, 2005). Having a strong vocabulary can equate to strong comprehension; however, vocabulary can also be taught or learned through reading comprehension. Although fluency helps with word reading recognition, students should be taught how to process what was read. In other words, utilizing previously taught foundational skills will assist in helping students to use comprehension strategies to fully understand text.

Table 5.2 Summary of Eight Dimensions of Comprehension

Dimension	Explanation
Connecting	☐ Make connections to the words by associating an image with the word ☐ Have a discussion about the word connecting it to prior knowledge or attaching a movement to the word
Inferring	☐ Help students to identify and define base words and word parts that change the meanings of words. ☐ Teach prefixes and suffixes that occur most frequently in words. ☐ Teach students to use word-part clues to figure out unfamiliar words. ☐ Teach most common Greek and Latin roots.
Visualizing	☐ Introduce and discuss a new concept. ☐ Have students brainstorm words they know related to the concept. ☐ Write words on a chart/map. ☐ Read related text, and then have students to discuss the text and add any new words to the chart/map. ☐ The teacher should have a series of questions prepared to guide the conversation.
Questioning	☐ Teach students multiple meaning words and how to use context clues to determine the correct meaning. ☐ Teach synonyms and antonyms of words. ☐ Use word walls and word banks to keep track of new words learned and encourage students to reference and use words in the conversations and writings. ☐ Teach figurative language and idioms.
Determining Importance	☐Use the Five Primary Dimensions of Fictional Texts ☐Have students create visualization graphic organizers
Synthesizing	☐Students should walk through: "*In the beginning I thought, then I thought, now, I am thinking*" model.
Predicting	☐ Allow students to make predictions before during and after interacting with text.
Summarizing	☐ One easy way to do this is to complete the "who, what, when, where, and how? Of the text.

Approach to Teaching Comprehension at Home

How many of you were not prepared to become full-time teachers over night? Well, as a former teacher, now principal, I was also unprepared for the shift. The Coronavirus pandemic changed the way we live immediately, and at some points, it appeared to be permanent. When it comes to comprehension, you are already equipped to develop your child's ability to read with comprehension, or true understanding. Feel free to sift back through this chapter to get an understanding of each strategy, as this section of the chapter was designed especially for you, to ensure your child's success.

Read, re-read, and keep reading with your child. Read-Alouds are a great instructional strategy to use at home. Based on the age and ability of your child, you may be required to read ahead and model the Read-Aloud, before you allow your child to read to you. Read with your child on a regular basis. Offer incentives to build excitement for reading. This can include, but is not limited to mommy/me dance offs, daddy/me workouts, no-chore passes, 15 minutes extended bedtime, or extra time on their favorite gaming system. The goal is to get children excited about reading.

Connecting

Connecting is one of the easier strategies to implement. Think of it like this, whatever your child is learning, you've experienced or witnessed at least once in your lifetime. Think about your favorite book and why it is your favorite. You can start by giving your child background information on the text, coupled with teaching text features (i.e., title, author, front/back cover, table of contents, and imagery, if applicable). Think about what your child can retain based on your connection to a text. Sharing common interests or beliefs with your child, can also help to excite them about reading.

Typically, when we talk about informational texts, we are focused on books, but one can also get information from the news, commercials, other individuals, social media, etc. Watching the news with your child can help them connect with content from all the disciplines (i.e., English/Language Arts (ELA), Mathematics, Science, and Social Studies). The news can assist with sentence structure and correct grammar in ELA, stocks and historical weather patterns in Math, weather, global warming, and pollen count in science, and lastly social justice, policies, voting, etc. in Social Studies; so, connecting the dots becomes easy. You can simply watch a portion of the news and ask follow up questions for each content area. Table 5.3 contains some sample questions for each content area. Additionally, you can help your child connect to the text by using sentence starters. See Figure 5.7 for examples of sentence starters to help your child use the connecting strategy.

Table 5.3 Sample Follow-Up Questions for Connecting in the Four Content Areas

Content Area	Sample Questions
ELA	☐ What's another way of saying what the reporter said? ☐ Can you put what the reporter said in your own words?
Math	☐ Based on the temperature today, was it warmer or cooler yesterday? ☐ What's the difference in the temperature?
Science	The meteorologist said it's raining tomorrow what will I need if I want to go outside?
Social Studies	☐ Racism is...what do you think we can do? ☐ Protesting is...what sign can we make to reflect our beliefs?

Figure 5.7 Examples of Sentence Starters for Connecting Strategy

☐ This reminds me of...
☐ I remember when...
☐ Something similar happened to me when...
☐ I can relate because...
☐ The setting reminds me of...
☐ I had the same feelings as...
☐ It reminds me of something in the world...
☐ This makes me think of the time when...
☐ This book reminds me of...

Allow your child to use these sentence starters to connect with the text based on their life experiences and background knowledge. By using these sentence starters, your child will learn how to connect text to self, text to text, text to world, and text to media. For example, after reading the picture book *When Sophie Gets Angry- Really Really Angry* (Bang, 1999) you can prompt your child to use the sentence starter "I had the same feeling as...". This will allow your child to connect and relate to the text. With the same text, you may allow your child to make other connections to themselves, the world, and other texts. By making connections to the text, you are setting a foundation for your child to be able to infer what is going on in the text.

Inferring

Inferring is all about reading between the lines of what is said and making sense of what is not said. The easiest way to teach this is to have a conversation about how you give instructions regarding chores around the house. For example, *"Erica, clean your room,"* sounds completely different from the first time you say it, compared to the fifth time you say it. Your voice body language potentially changes. Ask your child if there was a difference and to explain what the difference is. The inference might be something like: *"there was a level of frustration in your voice; the same words were used, but the meaning changed due to having to repeat yourself."*

When you are reading a book with or to your child, it's all in the questioning! When teaching this strategy, encourage your child to think more deeply about the text. One recommendation would be to pre-read the text so that you have a better understanding of it first. Table 5.4 lists questions that can be used with either fiction or non-fiction books.

Table 5.4 Inferring Questions for Fiction and Non-fiction books

Fiction Inference Questions	Non-fiction Inference Questions
☐ What was the most important part of the book? Why? ☐ How would you describe (main character)? What kind of person is he/she? What evidence from the text supports your beliefs? ☐ Did (main character) learn any lessons? ☐ Did (main character) change in the story? How?	☐ What can you learn from the picture that is not said in words? ☐ What are the author's opinions about this topic? ☐ What questions do you have about the topic? ☐ Based on the heading, what do you think this section or chapter will be about?

These questions whether fiction or non-fiction encourage deeper thinking. It might be fun to answer the questions before your child, to compare answers once he or she finishes. You can also use this technique with your favorite television show. If something is happening behind the scenes, you can rewind and ask specific questions to further engage your child.

When making an inference your child should understand how to use clues within the text and their own background knowledge to make an inference. If you want your child to practice making inferences, provide scenarios for them. For example, you might grab your keys, put on your shoes, walk near the door, and ask your child to make an inference. Your child might infer that you are leaving without you actually saying, "*It's time to go*". Use a chart like Figure 5.8 to help your child to develop inferences for the text they're reading.

Figure 5.8 Sample Inference Chart

Developing an Inference		
Clues from What was Read +	What I Already Knew (Background Knowledge) =	Inference

Visualizing

"Seeing is believing" takes on a new meaning with this strategy. The first suggested activity for teaching your child to visualize is a story wheel. The purpose of a story wheel is to help students visualize story elements and practice summarizing. This is a 2-for-1 activity. You can actually do this with your child. Have your child to draw a circle, with a smaller circle in the middle. Divide the outer circle into 6-8 equal parts (think about a pie with a small circle in the middle) then follow the steps listed in Figure 5.9. If you have multiple children, a great extension of this activity would be to share the story wheels and ask them what they think the story is about, based on the illustrations.

Figure 5.9 Visualization Story Wheel Activity

☐ Read the story. ☐ List important events (must include elements from the beginning, middle and end of the story). ☐ Determine the 6-8 most important events. ☐ Individuals can write, but for this activity, illustrate the events identified in the previous step. ☐ Add Title and Author to the middle of the smaller circle.	

The second activity is facilitating a Think-Aloud. The purpose of a Think-Aloud is to demonstrate when, why, and how to visualize while reading. The goal is for you to model how to create images, in your mind, when reading a text. Select a section from a text, to read aloud. As you are reading to your child, identify stopping points to share out loud what comes to mind as you read. Don't simply share what comes to mind, but also how and what led you to come to those thoughts. This includes personal stories and prior knowledge. The best way to do this is with use of your five senses (see, hear, feel, smell, taste). Lastly, explain to your child how creating the image in your head helped you to understand and connect to the text. If your child is a visual learner, allow them to draw pictures of whatever comes to mind as you read the text. When your child draws as you read, it will allow them to recall the information that was read. While your child draws, be sure to use questioning to ensure comprehension.

Questioning

The goal to questioning, is to do so, throughout the reading. This includes before, during, and after engaging with the text. The easiest way to do this is through questioning. Questioning activates children's thinking and increases their engagement. Questioning should take place before, during and after reading the text.

Before reading the text, show your child the front cover of a book and questioning them on what they think the book will be about. You can then ask a follow-up question like: "*why do you think that?*" During reading, you should pause to allow your child to process what was read through questioning. You may ask your child questions using *who, what, when, where, why, and how*.Asking questions while reading text gives the text meaning and allows your child to interact with the text.

Questioning at the end of a story can provide you with an understanding of how well your child processed the information in the text. This may be a fun time to discuss a change in the ending of the text or discuss the main idea of the text. Asking questions after reading allow your child to analyze what has been read and promotes comprehension of the text. This will also help your child to determine the importance of what was read. To read more in-depth research on questioning, refer to the section on questioning for teachers, but there are some examples of questions to use before, during, and after reading are listed here in Table 5.5.

Table 5.5 Before, During, and After Reading Question

Before Reading	During Reading	After Reading
☐ What do you think will happen? ☐ Why do you think...?	☐ I wonder why... ☐ What do you think about...? ☐ How come...? ☐ This reminds me of...?	☐ What would have happened if? ☐ I wonder why the author...? ☐ What message do you think the author wanted you to know?

Determining importance

Children must prioritize information as they read. Two primary components of determining importance is identifying themes (what message is the author sending) and identifying main ideas (differentiate between interesting and main ideas). This is based on the type of text being read. With this, let's think literally. This is a skill to be developed over time. Figure 5.10 gives a sample activity of how to determine importance.

Figure 5.10 Determining Importance Activity

Question: Tomorrow, you are going to school. What should go in your book bag?
Response: I need my cell phone, snacks, money, notebook, pen, paper, pencil and charger.
Rationale:
I used my 4th grade daughter and those were her responses. I then asked her to revisit the list to determine what was important. Her new list included pen, paper, notebook, and pencil. I asked her to explain why the list changed.

You can use this same activity for various locations that require specific items.

With the present civil unrest across the world, consider using the *I Have a Dream Speech,* by Dr. Martin Luther King, Jr. to teach how to your child how to identify theme. Start with asking your child what they know about Dr. Martin Luther King, Jr. Next, read the speech to them. If your child is of age, allow them to read it to you and ask questions for clarity. After gaining a general understanding of what is said, ask them what they think it means. In the event their responses align with civil rights, economic rights, equal rights for all, or the need to end racism, they have determined themes. In the event their responses don't align with those topics, just use questions from the previous section to assist in their understanding.

When determining importance, some children may require a visual. To help with this, get a sheet of paper and fold it in half. Have the child write what they think is important on one side and why they think those things are important on the other side. For children who are still learning to formulate sentences, allow them to make illustrations. The purpose of determining importance is to have the child develop a better understanding of the text as a whole.

Synthesizing

Parents, how many of you remember, hearing something (from a friend, child, or the radio) and having an immediate reaction, but once more information was shared, you changed your thinking? That's what synthesizing is: a change in one's thinking changing as more information is revealed and understood. Synthesizing in a fictional text requires students to break down their thinking of a text using the following three stems:

1. first, I was thinking
2. when I was reading, I was thinking
3. but at the end of the story, I am thinking...

Having a discussion around these three questions with your child can deepen their understanding of what they read.

The common fable, *The Tortoise and the Hare,* would be a great text to teach this strategy. Hint: Make sure whatever fable you choose; the lesson or theme is clear and age appropriate for your child. You should also ask questions linked to the theme or lesson of the text. To help with this, use a Double Bubble or Venn Diagram when reading non-fiction and determine ahead of time when students will respond to the three questions below to guide your child through this process:

1. What is the story about?
2. Is the story about anything else?
3. What's the lesson in the story?

Children should also be taught how to build on their knowledge when synthesizing. This can be modeled by using a pyramid to demonstrate the concept of building on previous knowledge or understanding. Use Figure 5.11 as a guide. In the top part of the pyramid, have your child write their first thoughts. The middle of the pyramid should be your child's thoughts as they read the story. The bottom of the pyramid should be their thoughts after the read the story. Please be sure to help your child to recall information as you work your way down the pyramid.

Figure 5.11 Synthesis Pyramid

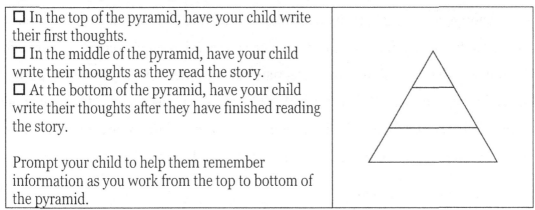

☐ In the top of the pyramid, have your child write their first thoughts.
☐ In the middle of the pyramid, have your child write their thoughts as they read the story.
☐ At the bottom of the pyramid, have your child write their thoughts after they have finished reading the story.

Prompt your child to help them remember information as you work from the top to bottom of the pyramid.

Predicting

Predictions are fairly easy to make. Essentially, you are guessing what will happen next, based on the information you have or what you believe. An activity is outlined in Figure 5.12.

Figure 5.12 Predicting Activity

☐ Tell your child they are a researcher.
☐ Have the child list the names of all family members and what they think their favorite item (candy, cookie, ice cream, flavor, etc.) is.
☐ Have the child ask each family member what their actual favorite item is.

What's most important, in this activity, is that your child compares their predictions to the actual responses. Depending on their age, you may want to ask them how they came up with their predictions (i.e., *every time we go to the store, my brother asks for...*).

An example with use of a text may require prepping (reading and/or skimming the text in advance). Based on the cover and the title, have the child predict what the book is about. This requires you to engage, on a consistent basis, with your child and the text. Before moving to the next page, ask them what they think will happen next and what led them to their thinking. Feel free to share with them what you think. You can use the same steps when watching television. The goal, throughout predicting, is to have the child think ahead, while helping them to comprehend the text.

Summarizing

Children must be able to put what they've read into their own words. The focus is solely on the main points of the text. Having your child to retell events is not enough. They have to have the ability to differentiate between the elements that are important and those that are not. The best question to start practicing this is: *"How was your day today at school?"* Your child's response should spark further discussion. Here are some questions that you should ask to have your child summarize their day:

1. What did you learn?
2. What new words did you learn? What do those words mean?
3. What class or event did you not like? Why?

Learners should also be encouraged to reread texts to ensure understanding. Rereading helps build fluency and develop vocabulary. As you are reading with your child, if there are any unknown words, place a box around them as an indicator that additional information is needed. If a word is read again, and the child is still unclear of its meaning, look it up together. To ensure understanding of the new word, place it in a new sentence that the two of you develop together.

Conclusion

"Comprehension strategies can be important to a reader because they have the potential to provide access to knowledge that is removed from personal experiences" (Stahl, 2004, p. 598). The goal of reading comprehension is to apply critical thinking strategies to develop proficient readers. Readers learn to read for skill when they use strategies such as connecting, inferring, visualizing, questioning, determining importance, synthesizing, predicting, and summarizing. These strategies combined with time, opportunity, and previous knowledge will build a metacognitive foundation for reading comprehension success. Teachers and parents can help children with comprehension by developing background knowledge, discussing the purpose of reading, modeling reading comprehension strategies, and providing students the additional support they need.

Comprehension is one's ability to understand something. To fully understand something, we must provide children with ample opportunities and experiences. When reading, comprehension is developed independently after a child has developed an understanding of phonemic awareness, phonics, vocabulary, and fluency. To prepare children for the comprehension of text, we must build upon their foundational skills.

Table 5.6 Additional Resources for Teaching Reading Comprehension

Title of Resource	URL	Description
Video *Who Wears Shoes?*	https://youtu.be/icnJThjlAQI	Building Comprehension by Making Inferences (Virtual Tour)
Reading Comprehension Strategy Series: How to Teach Determining Importance in the Upper Elementary Classroom	https://www.classroomnook.com/blog/determining-importance	Online resource with strategies for teaching readers how to determine importance.
Determining Importance	https://www.wayland.k12.ma.us/UserFiles/Servers/Server_1036352/File/Curriculum/Units%20of%20Study/Unit%20of%20study%20-%20Determining%20Importance.pdf	Lesson plans and strategies to teach students how to determine importance.
Book *Reading with Meaning* by Debbie Miller	Available on Amazon.com	This book assists with teaching synthesizing.
Book List	https://thisreadingmama.com/great-books-for-teaching-synthesizing/	List of books for teaching synthesizing.

Video Predicting and Inferring: Scaffolding Comprehension Strategies using an Explicit Framework	https://www.youtube.com/watch?v=ur6XREtI6ec#action=share	The facilitator models a scaffolded reasoning activity to teach predictions and inferences.
Reading Strategies and Misconceptions	https://readingstrategiesmsu.weebly.com/predicting.html	Strategies for teaching students predicting.
Video *Summary Map: Scaffolding Summary Writing*	https://www.youtube.com/watch?v=ur6XREtI6ec#action=share	In this video, the facilitator shares how students build essential skills in comprehension and develop a greater understanding of the structural features of a summary by creating a summary map.
Introduction to Summarize and Synthesize	https://readingrecovery.clemson.edu/summarize-and-synthesize/	Resource with strategies for teaching summarizing and synthesizing.
Video *Think-Alouds: Modeling Ways to Think about Text (Virtual Tour)*	https://www.youtube.com/watch?v=G0ZHimY5YZo	The facilitator models how to conduct an effective think-aloud.
Books	*The Important Book* by Margaret Wise Brown *Love Will See You Through* by Angela Farris Watkins *The Stray Dog* by Marc Simont *Grandfather's Journey* by Allen Say	These books will help with teaching comprehension.
Bridges for Kids – IEP Goals Bank	www.bridges4kids.org	This resource provides hundreds of examples of IEP goals and objectives.
Vocabulary	www.flocabulary.com	Hip-hop videos and instructional activities that promote literacy and spark creativity.

CHAPTER SIX

BONUS STRATEGIES

Socratic Seminar
This strategy allows students to learn and reflect from one another. This approach allows the students to give their perspectives, thoughts, and position when it comes to the content. The teacher supports this strategy by acting as a facilitator and providing scholars with different higher-order thinking questions. As a facilitator, the teacher can create a culture that focuses on collaboration and nurturing the scholar's voice and contributions. By having the scholars talk more, this allows them the ability to listen and adjust instructional delivery based on the perspectives and thoughts that are conveyed during the session. Also, this allows the scholars to own the classroom. The URL below links to a video where you can see how this strategy is implemented in the classroom. https://youtu.be/pQIiMT5O-jA
☐Phonemic Awareness ☐Phonics ☑Vocabulary ☐Fluency ☑Comprehension
Contributed by: Larue M. Fitch, M.Ed.
Quick, Informal Methods to Reinforce Reading at Home
☐ Read with the dictionary present to immediately look up any unfamiliar words ☐ Look for timelines in the passage (to make sure students understand the order in which things are happening). ☐ Ask the students questions while reading. ☐ Have student visualize the story by asking them to describe what is being read ☐ Have the student relate the story to people or places they know or would like to know more about
☐Phonemic Awareness ☐Phonics ☐Vocabulary ☑Fluency ☐Comprehension
Contributed by: Dr. Sheva Quinn
Express Yourself
☐ Have the learner think of how the character is feeling and how the learner would sound if she/he also felt that way. ☐Have learner try to match her/his voice with the feeling of the character. This strategy will help tremendously with expression. Also, this strategy should remind students that reading is a thinking process.
☐ Phonemic Awareness ☐ Phonics ☐ Vocabulary ☑Fluency ☐ Comprehension

Flip It

☐ Have the students ask themselves if the word looks and sounds right or if it makes sense.
☐ If the answer is no, have the student read the word again and try flipping the vowel sound (short or long).

☐ Phonemic Awareness	☑Phonics	☐ Vocabulary	☐ Fluency	☐

Comprehension

Contributed by: Quatia Stevens

Record Reading

☐Select a short story grade-level appropriate book.
☐ The parent or teacher reads the book to the student.
☐ Take each sentence from the book and write each word on an index card.
☐ Take one sentence, mix the cards up, and then place them on the table.
☐ Start the stopwatch to see how many cards the student can correctly read and pick up.
☐ Document the time.
☐ Repeat the same procedures for the second sentence and so forth.
☐ If the child reads a word incorrectly, flip it over on the table.
☐ Incorrect words can be pronounced by the parent or teacher during the last round.
☐ Start the stopwatch and have the student read the book to see if less time was used to read the book than reading the index cards.
☐ The goal is to use the index cards to improve reading fluency before the student reads the book.

☐Phonemic Awareness	☐Phonics	☐Vocabulary	☑Fluency

☐Comprehension

Contributed by: Dr. Tricia Y. Travis

Close Reading Strategies

Close Reading Strategies are used for enhancing critical thinking skills, vocabulary acquisition, and improving writing skills. This strategy is used for teaching students how to get past the main idea of a text and to break down the text for more critical analysis.

☐ Begin by practicing close reading an image, followed by close reading short articles, and then close reading full books.
☐ Text dependent questions should accompany any close reading lesson.
Each step should be practiced several times so students become familiar with the process of learning to annotate text. These steps include: circling words that are unfamiliar or that the student does not understand, underlining evidence to support the meaning of parts of the text, and learning how to write their own text-dependent questions.

Additional Resources on Close Reading Strategies:
☐   https://www.facinghistory.org/resource-library/teaching-strategies/close-reading-protocol
☐ www.scholastic.com
☐ www.com/close reading strategies

☐ Phonemic Awareness	☐ Phonics	☑Vocabulary	☑Fluency

☑Comprehension

Contributed by: Dee Harris

REFERENCES

Introduction

Covington, C. (2016). School improvement grants in Georgia: A quantitative analysis of the relationship between the college and career ready performance index, students' proficiency, and graduation rates. (ED571707). *Doctoral dissertation, Northcentral   University.* ProQuest Dissertations Publishing.

Green, E., & Goldstein, D. (2019, December). *Reading scores on national exam decline in half the states.* Retrieved July 6, 2020, from https://www.nytimes.com/2019/10/30/us/reading-scores-national-exam.html

Chapter One

Blachman, B. (2000). Phonological awareness. In M. L. Kamil, P. B. Rosenthal, P. D. Pearson, and R. Barr (eds.), *Handbook of reading research, 3,* 483-502. Mahwah, NJ: Erlbaum.

Blachman, B. (1995). Identifying the core linguistic deficits and the critical conditions for early intervention with children with reading disabilities. Paper presented at the annual meeting of the Learning Disabilities Association, Orlando, FL, March 1995.

Fingal, J. (2020). *Teach students how to read-and understand-digital text.* Retrieved June 12, 2020 from, https://www.iste.org/explore/learning-during-covid-19/teach-students-how-read-and-understand-digital-text.

Kamhi, A. (2007). Knowledge deficits: the true crisis in education. *ASHA Leader, 12*(7), *28–29.* Linda Farrell, Michael Hunter, and Tina Osenga are founding partners of Readsters, LLC.

Reade, A., & Sayko, S. (2017). *Learning about your child's reading development.* Washington, DC: U.S. Department of Education, Office of Elementary and Secondary Education, Office of Special Education Programs, National Center on Improving Literacy. Retrieved from http://improvingliteracy.org

Phonological and Phonemic Awareness. Reading Rockets. Retrieved June 12, 2020 from, https://www.readingrockets.org/reading-topics/phonological-and-phonemic-awareness .

Sheakoski, M. (2014). *What do phonics, phonemic awareness, and decoding mean?* Coffee Cups and Crayons. https://www.coffeecupsandcrayons.com/phonics-phonemic-awareness-decoding-mean/

Tankersley, K. (2003). *Threads of Reading.* Association for Supervision and Curriculum Development.

Chapter Two

Alfieri, L., Brooks, P., Aldrich, N., & Tenenbaum, H. (2011). Does discovery-based instruction enhance learning? *Journal of Educational Psychology, 103*, 1–18. doi:10.1037/a0021017

Aslin, R. (2017). Statistical learning: A powerful mechanism that operates by mere exposure. *Wiley Interdisciplinary Reviews: Cognitive Science, 8*, 1–7. doi:10.1002/wcs.1373

Castles, A., Rastle, K., & Nation, K. (2018). Ending the reading wars: Reading acquisition from novice to expert. *Psychological Science in the Public Interest, 19*, 5–51.

Evans, M., & Saint-Aubin, J. (2005). What children are looking at during shared storybook reading: Evidence from eye movement monitoring. *Psychological Science, 16*, 913–920. doi:10.1111/j.1467-9280.2005.01636.x

Gough, P., & Hillinger, M. (1980). Learning to read: An unnatural act. *Bulletin of the Orton Society, 30*, 179–196. doi:10.1007/BF0265371

Liberman, I., Shankweiler, D., Fischer, F., & Carter, B. (1974). Explicit syllable and phoneme segmentation in the young child. *Journal of Experimental Child Psychology, 18*, 201–212. doi:10.1016/0022-0965(74)90101-5

National Reading Panel. (2000, April). *Teaching Children to Read.* Retrieved from https://www.nichd.nih.gov/publications/pubs/nrp/findings

Shultz, S., & Vouloumanos, A. (2010). Three-month-olds prefer speech to other naturally occurring signals. *Language Learning and Development*, 6, 241–257. doi:10.1080/15475440903507830

Rudginsky, L., Haskell, E., & Rudginsky, L. 1997. *How to Teach Spelling.* Cambridge, Mass.: Educators Pub. Service.

Treiman, R. (2018). What Research Tells Us About Reading Instruction. *What Research Tells Us About Reading Instruction*, *19*(1), 1–4. https://doi.org/10.1177/1529100618772272

Chapter Three

Anderson, Richard C., & Others. (30 Nov. 1984). "Becoming a Nation of Readers: The Report of the Commission on Reading." *ERIC*, University of Illinois, Becoming a Nation of Readers, P.O. Box 2774, Station A, Champaign, IL 61820-8774, eric.ed.gov/?id=ED253865.

Beck, I., McKeown, M., & Kucan, L. (2013). Bringing words to life: Robust vocabulary instruction (2nd ed.). *New York: Guilford Press.*

Biemiller, A. (2005a). Size and sequence in vocabulary development: Implications for choosing words for primary words for primary grade vocabulary instruction. In E. H. Hiebert and M. L. Kamil (eds.), *Teaching and learning vocabulary: Bringing research to practice.* Mahwah, NJ: Erlbaum.

Biemiller, A. (2005b). Vocabulary development and instruction: A prerequisite for school learning. In D. Dickinson and S. Neuman (eds.), *Handbook of early literacy research, 2.* New York: Guilford.

Cabell, S., Justice, L., McGinty, A., DeCoster, J., & Forston, L. (2015). Teacher-child conversations in preschool classrooms: Contributions to children's vocabulary development. *Early Childhood Research Quarterly*, *30*(Pt. A, 1), 80-92. https://doi.org/10.1016/j.ecresq.2014.09.004

Cervetti, G., Hiebert, E., Pearson, P., & McCLung, N. (2015). Factors that influence the difficulty of science words. *Journal of Literacy Research*, *47*(2), 153-185. https://doi.org/10.1177/1086296X15615363

Cunningham, A., & Stanovich, K. (1998). What reading does for the mind. *American Educator, 22*, 8-15.

Edwards. E., G. Font, J. F. Baumann, & E. Boland. 2004. Unlocking word meanings: Strategies and guidelines for teaching morphemic and contextual analysis. In J. F. Baumann and E. J. Kame'enui (eds.), *Vocabulary instruction: Research to practice.* New York: Guilford.

raves, M., C. Juel, and B. B. Graves. 2004. *Teaching reading in the twenty-first century* (3rd ed.). Boston: Allyn & Bacon.

Hart, B., and T. R. Risley, 1995. *Meaningful differences in the everyday experience of young American children.* Baltimore, MD: Paul H. Brookes.

Henry, M. (2003). Unlocking literacy: *Effective decoding & spelling instruction.* Baltimore, MD: Paul H. Brookes.

Hiebert, E. (2020). The core vocabulary: The foundation of proficient comprehension. *The Reading Teacher, 73*(6), 757-768. International Literacy Association. https://doi.org/10.1002/trtr.1894.

Hiebert, E., Goodwin, A., & Cervetti, G. (2018). Core vocabulary: Its morphological content and presence in exemplar texts. *Reading Research Quarterly, 53*(1), 29-49. https://doi.org10.1002/rrq.183

Honig, B., Diamond, L., Cole, C., & Gutlohn, L. (2008). *Teaching reading sourcebook: For all educators working to improve reading achievement* (2nd ed.). Novato, CA: Arena Press.

Marzano, R., & Marzano, J. (1988). *A cluster approach to elementary vocabulary instruction.* Newwark, DE: International Reading Association.

Marzano, R., & Simms, J. (2013, June 14). *Vocabulary for the Common Core, Tips.* Marzano Resources. Retrieved June 2, 2020, from https://www.marzanoresources.com/resources/tips/vcc_tips_archive

Nagy, W., & Hiebert, E. (2011). Toward a theory of word selection. In M.L. Kamil, P.D. Pearson, E.B. Moje, & P.P. Afflerbach (Eds.), *Handbook of reading research, 4,* 388-404. New York, NY: Longman.

National Reading Panel: Teaching children to read: An evidence-based assessment of the scientific research literature on reading and its implications for reading instruction: Reports of the subgroups. (2000). Washington, D.C.?: National Institute of Child Health and Human Development, National Institutes of Health.

O'Connor, R. (2007). *Teaching word recognition: Effective strategies for children with learning difficulties.* Guilford.

Scharer, P. (2018). *Responsive literacy: A comprehensive framework.* New York, Scholastic, Incorporated.

Scharer, P. (2018). *Responsive literacy: A comprehensive framework*. New York, Scholastic, Incorporated.

Southall, M. (2011). *Differentiating reading instruction for success with RTI: Grades K-3*. Scholastic.

Southall, M. (2011). *Differentiating reading instruction for success with RTI: Grades K-3*. Scholastic.

Stahl, S. (2005). Four problems with teaching word meanings (and what to do to make vocabulary an integral part of instruction). In E. H.Hiebert and M. L. Kamil (eds.), *Teaching and learning vocabulary: Bringing research to practice*. Mahwah, NJ: Erlbaum.

Stahl, S., and W. E. Nagy. (2000). *Promoting vocabulary development*. Austin, Texas Education Agency.

White, T., J. Sowell, and A. Yanagihara. (1989). Teaching elementary children to use word-part clues. *Reading Teacher, 42*, 302-308.

"*Why Reading Aloud to Kids Helps Them Thrive (2020, July 20)*." PBS, Public Broadcasting Service. www.pbs.org/parents/thrive/why-reading-aloud-to-kids-helps-them-thrive.

Wright, T., & Cervetti, G. (2017). A systematic review of the research on vocabulary instruction that impacts text comprehension. *Reading Research Quarterly, 52*(2), 203-226. https://doi.org/10.1002/rrq.163

Chapter Four

Baker, L., Dreher, M., & Guthrie, J. (2000). *Engaging young readers: Promoting achievement and motivation*. Guilford Press.

Bender, W., & Larkin, M. (2003). *Reading Strategies for Elementary Students with Learning Difficulties. Thousand Oaks*, Corwin Press.

Flora, S. B. (2007). *The Best Sight Word Book Ever!, Grades K - 3: Learn 170 High-Frequency Words and Increase Fluency and Comprehension Skills*.

Griffith, P. L. (2008). *Literacy for Young Children: A Guide for Early Childhood Educators. Thousand Oaks*, Corwin Press.

Homan, S., Klesius, J., & Hite, C. (1993). Effects of Repeated Readings and Nonrepetitive Strategies on Students' Fluency and Comprehension. *The Journal of Educational Research, 87*(2), 94-99.

Knoll, E. (2015). *Using Echo Reading and Tracking Simultaneously during Small Group Read-Alouds with Preschool Children.*

Kuhn, M., & Levy, L. (2015). *Developing Fluent Readers: Teaching Fluency as a Foundational Skill.*

LaBerge, D., & Samuels, S. (1974). Toward a Theory of Automatic Information Processing in Reading. *Cognitive Psychology, 6*(2), 293-323.

Lapp, D., & Moss, B. (2012). *Exemplary Instruction in the Middle Grades: Teaching that Supports Engagement and Rigorous Learning.* Guilford Press.

Lems, K., Miller, L., & Soro, T. (2017). *Building literacy with English language learners: Insights from linguistics.*

Mackenzie, S. (2018). *The read-aloud family: Making meaningful and lasting connections with your kids.* Zondervan.

Mink, Deborah, V. (2009). *Strategies for Building Fluency.* Shell Education.

O'Connor, R. (2014). *Teaching word recognition: Effective strategies for students with learning difficulties.* Guilford Press.

Paige, D. (2011). "That Sounded Good!": Using Whole-Class Choral Reading to Improve Fluency. *The Reading Teacher, 64*(6), 435-438.

Rasinski, T. (2006). Reading Fluency Instruction: Moving Beyond Accuracy, Automaticity, and Prosody. *The Reading Teacher, 59*(7), 704-706.

Rasinski, T. (2005). The Fluent Reader: Oral Reading Strategies for Building Word Recognition, Fluency, and Comprehension. Scholastic Professional Books.

Rasinski, T., Blachowicz, C., & Lems, K. (2012). *Fluency Instruction: Research-based Best Practices.* Guilford Press.

Rasinski, T., & Padak, N. (2013). *From fluency to comprehension: Powerful instruction through authentic reading.*

Stanovich, K. (2000). *Progress in Understanding Reading: Scientific Foundations and New Frontiers.* Guilford Press.

Stuart, M., & Stainthorp, R. (2016). *Reading development & teaching.* Sage Publications Ltd.

Williams, R., & Giordano, C. (2019). *Read to your baby every day: 30 classic nursery rhymes to read aloud*. Frances Lincoln Children's Books.

Chapter Five

Alexander, F. (2020). *Understanding vocabulary*. Retrieved May 19, 2020, from https://www.scholastic.com/teachers/articles/teaching-content/understandingvocabulary/

Bailey, E. (2015). *Reading comprehension skills: Making predictions*. Retrieved May 28, 2020 from http://specialed.about.com/od/readingliteracy/a/Reading-Comprehension-Skills Making-Predictions.htm

Bang, M. (1999). *When Sophie gets Angry- Really, Really, Angry*. Scholastic.

Beers, K. (2003). *When kids can't read: What teachers can do*. Heinemann.

Boyle, J. (2014). The effects of a Venn diagram strategy on the literal, inferential, and relational comprehension of students with mild disabilities. *Learning Disabilities: A Multidisciplinary Journal, 10*(1). Retrieved from https://js.sageamorepub.com/ldmj/article/view/5404

Carr, E., & Ogle, D. (1987, April). Summarizing K-W-L plus: A strategy for comprehension and summarization. *Journal of Reading, 30*(7), 626-631.

Gunning, T. (2012). *Creating literacy instruction for all children in grades pre-K to 4*. 2nd Edition. A and B.

Harvey, S., & Goudvis, A. (2017). *Strategies that work: Teaching comprehension for understanding, engagement, and building knowledge, grades K-8* (3rd edition). Stenhouse Publishers.

Ludwig, T., & Barton, P. (2013). *The invisible boy*. Alfred A. Knopf.

Marzano, R. (2010). Teaching inference. *Educational Leadership, 67*(7), 80-01.

Meltzer, B., & Eliopoulos, C. (2017). *I am Martin Luther King, Jr*. Scholastic Inc.

Miller, D. (2013). *Reading with meaning*. Stenhouse Publishers.

Ozgungor, S., & Guthrie, J. (2004). Interactions among elaborative interrogation, knowledge, and interest in the process of constructing knowledge from text. *Journal of Educational Psychology, 96*(3), 437-443.

Rania, Tusa, T., & DiPucchio, K. (2012). *The sandwich swap*. CNIB.

Schweinhart, L., Montie, J., Xiang, Z., Barnett, W., Belfield, C., & Nores, M. (2005).*Lifetime effects: The High/Scope Perry Preschool study through age 40.* (Monographs of the High/Scope Educational Research Foundation, 14). High/Scope Press.

Shanahan, T., & Shanahan, C. (2012). What is disciplinary literacy and why does it matter? *Top Language Disorders, 32*(1), 7-18.

Shea, M., & Ceprano, M. (2017). Reading with understanding: A global expectation. *Journal of Inquiry & Action in Education, 9*(1), 48-68.

Stahl, K. (2004, April). Proof, practice, and promise: Comprehension strategy instruction in   the primary grades. *The Reading Teacher, 57*(7), 598-609.

Trehearne, M., & Healy, L. (2005). *Comprehensive literacy resource for grades 1-2 teachers.*
ETA Cuisenaire.

Wilson, D. (2014, May). *Brain movies; When readers can picture it, they understand it.*
Retrieved May 21, 2020, from https://www.edutopia.org/blog/brain-movies-visualizereading-comprehension-donna-wilson

Zygouris-Coe, V. (2009). *Teaching Reading Comprehension Skills.* NAESP Middle Matters.

Made in the USA
Columbia, SC
10 December 2024

47756356R00076